# WASHING WINDOWS IV

*honouring*

JOAN MCBREEN
*Poet. Trailblazing Editor*

JESSIE LENDENNIE
*Writer. Visionary Publisher*

SIOBHAN HUTSON
*Artist. Genius Designer*

# WASHING WINDOWS IV
*Irish Women Write Poetry*

Alan Hayes and Nuala O'Connor
*editors*

ARLEN
HOUSE

WASHING WINDOWS IV
*Irish Women Write Poetry*

is published in 2024 by
ARLEN HOUSE
42 Grange Abbey Road
Baldoyle
Dublin D13 A0F3
Ireland
arlenhouse@gmail.com
arlenhouse.ie

978–1–85132–333–3, *paperback*

Distributed internationally by
SYRACUSE UNIVERSITY PRESS
621 Skytop Road, Suite 110
Syracuse
New York
13244–5290
USA
supress@syr.edu
syracuseuniversitypress.syr.edu

poems © individual authors, 2024
selection/preface © Alan Hayes, 2024
afterword © Nuala O'Connor, 2024

The moral right of the authors has been reserved

Typesetting by Arlen House

cover image: 'Reaching for Alder Branches'
by Pauline Bewick
watercolour • 2004

## Contents

9   *Why Washing Windows?*

11  *Poetry – Power, Politics, Patronage and Privilege*
    Alan Hayes

17  *In the Shadows and Accidents*
    Nuala O'Connor

WASHING WINDOWS IV
25  Maeve Abyss / *Bluetooth*
27  Síle Agnew / *Fractures*
28  Michelle Ivy Alwedo / *International Student*
29  Marie Bashford-Synnott / *Writing Life*
30  Trish Bennett / *Port na bPúcaí*
33  Claire Blennerhassett / *Pivot*
35  Sara Boyce / *Revelation*
36  Yvonne Boyle / *Catastrophic Loss of Function*
38  Caroline Bracken / *Bon Voyage*
39  Marie Breen-Smyth / *The Secret of a Long Life*
40  Clodagh Brennan Harvey / *'And the Winner Is ...'*
41  Jacquie Burgess / *Call and Response*
43  Lynn Caldwell / *Lonely is Just One Letter Away from Lovely*
44  Mary Rose Callaghan / *Resuscitation*
46  Marion Clarke / *Slowing Down*
47  Susan Condon / *First Dance*
49  Martina Dalton / *To Raise a Writing Room*
51  Maureen Daly / *Be Courageous*
52  Sorcha de Brún / *Rialacha Cogaidh*
54  Helen Dempsey / *Jane Donnelly*
55  Doreen Duffy / *Things are Getting Ready to Happen*

| | |
|---|---|
| 56 | Ger Duffy / *Teratogen* |
| 58 | Catherine Dunne / *Old Photographs* |
| 60 | Micheline Egan / *Not Linear or Elegant* |
| 62 | Attracta Fahy / *Opposing Opposites* |
| 63 | Helen Fallon / *Sierra Leone Saturdays* |
| 64 | Carole Farnan / *Seven Different Ways of Looking at Poets* |
| 66 | Tanya Farrelly / *Painting my Grandmother's Nails* |
| 67 | Deirdre Flaherty Brady / *Elegy to my Literary Foremothers* |
| 68 | Bernadette Fox / *The Everyday Fantastic* |
| 69 | Amy Gaffney / *The Breaking Point of a Writer*, or *Imposter Syndrome* |
| 71 | Shauna Gilligan / *I Left my Womb in Napoli* |
| 72 | Aimee Godfrey / *In Which my Grandfather is Played by Eugene Levy* |
| 73 | Anita Gracey / *Aunt Beatrice* |
| 74 | Angela Graham / *Do Unto Others* |
| 75 | Mim Greene / *Doorway* |
| 76 | Anita Greg / *The Mayday Wyrtsong* |
| 78 | Sinéad Griffin / *The Phillumenist* |
| 79 | Sharon Guard / *The Middle Age* |
| 80 | Christine Hammond / *Flight Path* |
| 81 | Rachel Handley / *They* |
| 82 | Phyl Herbert / *Outburst* |
| 84 | Florence Heyhoe / *In Good Spirits* |
| 85 | Jennifer Horgan / *Body* |
| 86 | Sacha Hutchinson / *1980 to 1986* |
| 88 | Jean James / *I was Small* |
| 90 | Rosemary Jenkinson / *Heliophile* |
| 92 | Cath-Ann Kavanagh / *Silent Treatment* |
| 93 | Hannah Kiely / *She, Braver than I* |
| 94 | Thérèse Kieran / *To a Poet* |
| 95 | Bethan Kilfoil / *Defibrillator* |
| 96 | Susan Knight / *Visions of a Thief of Night* |
| 98 | Donna Leamy / *Thalassophile* |

| | |
|---|---|
| 99 | Róisín Leggett Bohan / *The Path* |
| 100 | Mary Lockhart / *Poetry in Motion* |
| 101 | Jackie Lynam / *Glass of Poison* |
| 102 | Carmel Lynch / *The Embrace* |
| 104 | Noelle Lynskey / *The Voice Keeper* |
| 105 | Siobhán Mac Mahon / *Paving the Way* |
| 107 | Colette McAndrew / *Gone to Earth* |
| 108 | Catherine McCabe / *Fatso* |
| 109 | Mary McCarthy / *Invoke a Whisper* |
| 110 | Helen McClements / *Missed Co-Ordinates* |
| 113 | Raquel McKee / *Wet Quavers* |
| 114 | E.V. McLoughlin / *I Am Not Here* |
| 116 | Liz McManus / *To Ilhan Sami Çomak* |
| 117 | Eilís Ní Anluain / *Do Ilhan Sami Çomak* |
| 118 | Triona Mc Murrow / *The Rag Bag* |
| 119 | Patricia Maguire / *Enda* |
| 122 | Mari Maxwell / *On Soldier's Mountain* |
| 124 | Amanda Moloney / *Yule Eve* |
| 125 | Sonya Mulligan / *The Revolution Will Be Televised* |
| 127 | Mitzie Murphy / *Don't Tell* |
| 128 | Anne Murray / *Nearly Me* |
| 130 | Bríd Ní Chomáin / *Waiting on a Text* |
| 133 | Ciara Ní É / *Untitled* |
| 134 | Helena Nolan / *Iceland* |
| 135 | Maria Noonan-McDermott / *The Red Chair* |
| 137 | Grace O'Doherty / *Declination of Beauty* |
| 138 | Lauren O'Donovan / *To Mrs Brown, my Fifth-Year Biology Teacher* |
| 140 | Bláithín O'Reilly Murphy / *My First Born* |
| 141 | Sarah Padden / *How to Commit Genocide* |
| 143 | Celina Papendorf / *You* |
| 145 | Saakshi Patel / *Banu* |
| 146 | Ruth Quinlan / *A Poet's Inscription* |
| 147 | Mary Ringland / *Wooed* |
| 148 | Rebecca Ruane / *A 28-Year-Old-Woman Buys a Field in Galway* |
| 151 | D'or Selfer / *My 100th Attempt at a Love Poem* |

152 Mary Shannon / *On the Fourteen-Forty-Five Iarnród Éireann to Malahide*
153 Katie Sheehan / *Benediction*
154 Cassie Smith-Christmas / *Tahlequah J35*
155 Amy Smyth / *Still*
156 Eilis Stanley / *A Dangerous Thing*
158 Sarah Strong / *Billy's Room*
159 Lila Stuart / *Your Way*
160 Csilla Toldy / *Midsummer Reunion in Four Chapters*
163 Enya Trofimoff / *Rosemary Breath*
164 Carmel Uí Cheallaigh / *Dreoilín Dreoilín Rí na nÉan*
165 Emi Uyematsu / *Sitting Down in the Shower*
166 Morgan L. Ventura / *Spolia*

168 *About the Contributors*

## Why Washing Windows?

Catherine Rose/Eavan Boland, 1980s

In 1984, Catherine Rose, Arlen House's publisher, and Eavan Boland, Arlen's associate editor, founded the national organisation for Irish women writers, Women's Education Bureau (WEB), to develop workshops, mentorship and supportive and safe creative spaces for women.

Eavan Boland travelled Ireland hosting workshops and mentoring emerging women writers. At one event a poet told Eavan she was reluctant to 'go public' with her creative work. She felt she couldn't tell her neighbours she was a poet – because they would think that she didn't wash her windows.

That is the space and the culture which Eavan Boland, Catherine Rose and their sister feminists subverted and exploded. The vast array of Irish women writers today, reaching international heights, owe a debt of gratitude to these trailblazers for their radical work revolutionising Irish writing and the literary scene. Now Irish writing is a more diverse and open space, for both women and men, because of the truly groundbreaking and perilous work started by visionaries like Eavan Boland and Catherine Rose. Let us never forget. Let us never write their work out of history.

# POETRY
# POWER, POLITICS, PATRONAGE AND PRIVILEGE

Alan Hayes

These 100 new poems which comprise *Washing Windows IV* once again give us great hope for the future of Irish poetry. Selected from almost 1000 poems submitted to Arlen House by women who have yet to publish a full collection, I had challenging choices to make. So, while many poets didn't make it this time, it is heartening to know that the poetic talent out there by emerging female authors is immense.

Here are the voices who will shape a new poetry world. These writers come from all parts of the island and beyond, and write in English and *as Gaeilge*. They range in age over eight decades, and, as with all Arlen House anthologies, diversity is integrated throughout, in all its glory and in all its honesty. There are strong familial and community ties here. Many of these women have contributed to Ireland's cultural life for decades as prose writers, playwrights and visual artists. All have an interest in poetry, often from the days when an interest was not encouraged or welcomed. Thus, this anthology is representative of a new society, and a new way of accepting and honouring the talent all around us.

Though it has not always been so.

Women who are poets have not always been accepted or welcomed on equal terms. Talent has not always been the key factor. Power structures operate in dark corners.

There certainly have been better times for female poets in Ireland's literary history. The nineteenth century was, relatively, a golden time for Irish women writers. Anne Colman, in truly groundbreaking research undertaken in pre-internet days, discovered over 700 women writing poetry during the 1800s. In ongoing research, I have discovered over 100 Irish women who published poetry during the twentieth century who have yet to be 'reclaimed'.

However, it is clear from the 1950s onwards that conservative powerbrokers chose to champion their male peers and, in most instances, female voices were silenced. Often with the support of funders. I believe there were always female voices who could be silenced. There still are.

September 1975: Arlen House – Ireland's pioneering first feminist press – was established by Catherine Rose, a young Cork woman living in Galway. She gathered together a small group of other extraordinary women, including emerging poet Eavan Boland, who brought visionary ideas and practical help, and feminist activist and seer, Dr Margaret Mac Curtain, one of the leading voices campaigning for equality in society.

I believe all women writing today owe a debt of gratitude to these trailblazing women who were the first to open doors, at a time when it was difficult and dangerous to do so. They started a new creative movement, demanding a space, a voice and a vision for women. Thus commenced a new flowering, which we witness today in an ongoing renaissance of renowned female voices.

Though it may not always be so.

Unless systemic changes are made and enforced, progressive improvements in equality and diversity can always be dismantled. Power systems operate by twisted untruths. Recent Ministers for Arts have successfully delivered large increases in arts funding, thus many projects centered on the current 'diversity' buzzword have rightfully been supported. Though whether all grantees are genuine supporters of equality and diversity is a question that needs to be interrogated publicly. And what will happen when budget cuts come again? Will the decision-makers revert back to prioritising the old power structures – which traditionally had a poor record of equality and diversity?

Artistic organisations have existed with particular specialisms in equality and diversity, but then had their funding either cut, or completely abolished, when funding bodies faced with budget cuts made poor choices. The Arts Council/An Chomhairle Ealaíon, in particular, needs to be monitored closely. While Arlen House has the longest track record in equality, I do not believe that the Arts Council is a safe space creatively or culturally. As I have already said publicly, I believe the Arts Council needs to be invited to appear in front of the Public Accounts Committee of Dáil Éireann to answer questions regarding allocations of public funding. There are many questions that demand answers. As we witnessed over the past year of the RTÉ scandal, with multiple appearances by RTÉ executives and board representatives, it can take tenacious questioning for truths to be revealed.

This year I am delighted once again to invite Nuala O'Connor to co-edit *Washing Windows IV*. In her vivid introduction she reflects on the power and importance of poetry and considers many of the fascinating themes emerging in this anthology. 2024 marks the 21st anniversary of Nuala's first collection, and the publication of *Seaborne*, her 6th novel and 16th book. Arlen House was privileged to introduce one of the most original and important voices of twenty-first century literature. In 2003, the poetry world was vastly different to today. It was a space that was not as open and welcoming to women, at least as professional writers. I remember one young female poet saying she was told by an editor, patronisingly and condescendingly, that there was not one line of poetry in her manuscript – an opinion that awards judges, media reviewers and a large audience utterly disagreed with.

Diversity was not even a buzzword in the artistic lexicon then, despite the fact that equality legislation had recently been enacted by the government, and equality and diversity measures should have been implemented by all powerbrokers and decision-makers. It is inexplicable why it took so long, and disturbing when, at times, it is done so ineptly now. Often, Jessie Lendennie at Salmon Poetry remained a lone beacon advocating for progress and change in the poetry world. And sometimes a price had to be paid for doing so. Powerful publishers in the western world continued their long-standing exclusionary practices, often with public support and the approval of funding bodies; in Ireland the output of poetry presses, generally, was not reflective of modern society.

But the growing body of women poets, many of whom emerged from Arlen House/Eavan Boland's pioneering WEB workshops which commenced over 40 years ago, demanded opportunities; they refused to be silenced or sidelined. Thus came a new beginning for poetry in both the English and Irish languages. With the right supports, independent management, and honest engagement by the entire arts world, this is the perfect time to create opportunities for growth and blossoming.

Will that happen? Power structures remain stubbornly resistant to real change. We are told 'change takes time' – though nobody explains why that is so. And why do *we* allow it to be so? Over recent decades, the Irish poetry world has become increasingly younger, female and more diverse; a fact not represented adequately by powerbrokers and decision-makers. Tokenism is not acceptable. Not any longer.

This anthology honours the forementioned Jessie Lendennie, visionary editor and publisher at Salmon Poetry since 1981, and her colleague Siobhan Hutson who has been an integral part of Salmon's survival, growth and success for more than 30 years. We also honour pioneering poet Joan McBreen, whose first collection appeared almost 35 years ago and who continues to contribute to Ireland's literary heritage. Most especially we acknowledge Joan's groundbreaking anthology, *The White Page : An Bhileog Bhán: Twentieth-Century Irish Women Poets*, which Salmon published in 1999 as we now celebrate its 25th birthday. We look forward to a new edition which would document the vast development and expansion of opportunities for new women poets over the past quarter century – a movement that Salmon Poetry and Arlen House, in particular, have played substantial roles in creating and developing. *Washing Windows* acknowledges Jessie's, Siobhan's and Joan's visionary, brave and extraordinary contributions to Irish life and culture over many decades.

For recommendations, advice and wisdom, my thanks to Donal Ryan, Mary Coll and Jessie Lendennie.

And for now, and for ever, let us raise our voices to celebrate these 100 new poets, help them on their journeys and watch as they bring new vitality into Irish and international creative life.

And let it always be so.

# IN THE SHADOWS AND ACCIDENTS

## Nuala O'Connor

What do I – as reader – want from a poem? For me, I want my understanding to be stretched so far that it lands on fresh ground, and I want to encounter language that thrills me on that journey. I want, as Edna O'Brien says about all reading, to be brought 'to the frontiers of feeling' by a poem – I like a heart-grip of full emotion. I hope to find a landscape, or inner-scape, that I have never encountered before, with the poem as oblique or pointed map, where I can wander and explore. I like to be brought to places that feel both strange and familiar; I treasure the poems that give me a spinning compass and unsure ground, but that guide me well, too, helping me, in the end, to land on *terra firma*.

    Poetry, as we know, is used infrequently but triumphantly by most people on big occasions, to underline pertinent points to do with love, memory, grief, and more. And that is a beautiful, worthy thing. But for those immersed in it, poetry is often a daily companion, a place of learning and comfort. Poems let us, as writers, tackle our inner wash and backswash; as readers, those hooked on poetry find insight, knowledge, and hope in the verses we consume. We witness what is current and enraging in the world, what is hopeful and new. Poems teach us often how to make sense of it all, how to *be*.

The late, great Eavan Boland, one of our most valued poetry foremothers, said that:

> poetry begins where language starts: in the shadows and accidents of one person's life. If a poet does not tell the truth about time, his or her work will not survive it. Past or present, there is a human dimension to time, human voices within it, and human griefs ordained by it.

The poets in this volume are fearless in that project, they weave and truth-tell gloriously, capturing the vagaries and beauties of their moment. They consider love, of course, but also migration, violence, betrayal, and death; all the woes of our self-bludgeoned world. These are poems where wombs bleed out into Italian toilets; where mothers are respected and loved fiercely; and where one courageous, newly-enlightened poet – Angela Graham – proclaims: 'I am my Gorgon. I must turn to meet my stare ...'

In 1981, at an Irish Studies conference in Canada, Lorna Reynolds, in her keynote speech, said that:

> the women of Ireland, whether we look for them in legend, literature or life, do not correspond to the stereotypes that have, so mysteriously, developed in the fertile imaginations of men.

Forty plus years on and Irish women's writing is arguably in a healthier state thanks to intrepid female writers and to publishers, investments, schemes, and organisations that – at last – let women writers have their say, that take us seriously. Women who write have always respected themselves; have known that they can use their power to organise the world, and their words to improve it. Anthologies like this one prove that, given the right chance, such work can be brought to the light, to declare that we are no longer willing to be male-gazed into history – we insist on speaking for ourselves and on being heard.

French writer Hélène Cixous urged women writers to mine their own lives and bodies for inspiration. 'Write yourself,' she exhorted. The writers in this anthology are all for that and poet Micheline Egan obeys Cixous' tenet beautifully in her instructive elegy 'Not Linear or Elegant'. She writes, 'Prepare for clumsy/prepare for shock/and be careful about who's listening,/you do not want their/ competitive grief/as you search the world for balm/to soften your sandblasted heart.'

Like Egan, the other poets in *Washing Windows IV* are clear-eyed in their project of reflecting our selfhood, our community, and our planet back at us. And they are upfront, letting us know that what we see will not always be pretty. In 'International Student', Michelle Avy Alwedo finds snakes in the greener pastures of Ireland, giving a discerning look at how this country is perceived by those who come here; Alwedo slices through the shamrock haze to what is, nowadays, the truer picture: waning Irish hospitality. In 'Revelation' Sara Boyce treads similar ground with a moving poem about immigration to Ireland, where a disconnected woman, at the mercy of bureaucrats, 'feels her life ebb, slip its flimsy mooring'. Sarah Padden's urgent, powerful prose poem 'How to Commit Genocide' lays out the horrors of a present-day war and its modern tactics: 'When the ambassador cries at the UN Council because a girl called *Dunia*, whose name means the *realm of the whole world* was orphaned and pulled from rubble when her home was bombed, still had hope of a life even after her leg was amputated, but was killed a few weeks later in her hospital bed – cut the internet and power lines. Stop local journalists interviewing children for CNN and silence the poet.'

In an era obsessed with treadmilling and accumulation, despite all signs that opposite actions are needed, Claire Blennerhassett writes of radical personal renewal. In her poem 'Pivot', she talks of upheaving to return to a freer self, possibly an ancient way of being. 'Fall away the rickety scaffold/,' she writes, 'the leaning tower of *so much stuff*/that seeks to drag you, unrelenting,/towards a gravity not of your own.' Blennerhassett's narrator craves a simpler, truer life, one of kindness, closer to the older Irish lifestyle that we so casually and callously bury, in the name of modernity and, alleged, progress. As a culture we ignore the lessons in these important poems at our peril.

Many of these writers look for succour in the natural world, finding comfort in 'the moon's soft filament' as in Christine Hammond's piece. Or in Jean James' poem where she treasures the memory of the 'green womb of bracken' where she hid as a child. They remember passed away friends, as in Patricia Maguire's stunning 'Enda'; they honour in Irish and English, a poet-prisoner in Turkey, İlhan Sami Çomak. Fittingly, Siobhán Mac Mahon has a beautiful poem here about the death of Eavan Boland, and her grief as fellow poet; in it she 'marvels at the way/you might put the words/for poet and great and woman//into a single sentence/that burns a hole in the dark/history of her country.'

Carole Farnan in her lovely 'Seven Different Ways of looking at Poets' has writers as pan-handlers 'chasing that elusive gleam' and, also, as 'magpie linguists' who steal 'shiny words'. By contrast Jennifer Horgan writes, 'We, who are made/of welt and broken surfaces, leak our bodies/in assonance. Scream, until we are trapped/inside half-dying shells again, no longer trapped/in beds, kitchens, in laundries, in prisons,/not in asylums, or in convents, but in our own/poems.' Enclosed in poems, perhaps, but free too because the poets in *Washing Windows IV,* by releasing themselves onto the page, are now roaming the consciences of those who read this book.

Those readers will find that the panhandled gleams of these writers' life-accidents shine and reflect brightly, and many shadows are made abundantly clear.

Books by Nuala O'Connor/Nuala Ní Chonchúir

*Seaborne* (Dublin, New Island, 2024)
*Nora* (USA, Harper Collins/Dublin, New Island, 2021)
*Birdie* (Arlen House/Bowen Day Press, 2020)
*Becoming Belle* (USA, GP Putnam/Penguin Canada/UK, Little, Brown, 2018)
*Joyride to Jupiter* (New Island, 2017)
*Miss Emily* (USA, Penguin USA/UK, Sandstone, 2015)
*The Closet of Savage Mementos* (New Island, 2014)
*Of Dublin and Other Fictions* (USA, Tower Press, 2013)
*Mother America* (New Island, 2012)
*The Juno Charm* (Salmon Poetry, 2011)
*You* (New Island, 2010)
*Portrait of the Artist with a Red Car* (UK, Templar Poetry, 2009)
*Nude* (UK, Salt, 2009)
*Tattoo: Tatú* (Arlen House, 2007)
*To the World of Men, Welcome* (Arlen House, 2005/2011)
*The Wind Across the Grass* (Arlen House, 2004/2009)
*Molly's Daughter* in *Divas! New Irish Women's Writing* (Arlen House, 2003)

# Washing Windows IV

Maeve Abyss

## BLUETOOTH

I thought I got rid of you
but your fucking speaker name
still shows when I use Bluetooth

and the photos, fuck
the dinners you cooked
the trips that we took

I'm running out of storage
so I deleted you

I wanted to download a new app
designed to reduce anxiety
but your data was taking up room

I thought I got rid of you
but my call log from June
says that's not true

left over in the cloud
all my fears and doubts
which I've scoured now

erased videos of you singing
to swans on a lake
near your mom's

voice messages
about your thoughts on dreams
and god

I no longer want to keep you
in fact I release you
a midnight memory assassin
ate up the gigabytes all
the while laughing

a world of know everythings
but we don't know what
to do

heartbreak goes away
with no
digital proof

Síle Agnew

## Fractures

i

My uncle hungers for heated debate
throwing verbal grenades to the table
"SHE'S A SLUT!"

ii

An aunt with too much whiskey
chews on the bones of aggression,
her words drenched in venom.

iii

Raised voices ricochet through shocked silence.
A rainstorm of hurt feelings drip
down the walls like condensation.

iv

Weapons of words hit the target,
dead clouds of despair hang over the table
and kick the corpse of hope to dust.

Michelle Ivy Alwedo

## INTERNATIONAL STUDENT

It's safer there than here:
their sentiment of hate is clear.
My speaking manner, frizzy hair
and skin colour announces me as a foreigner.

The strangers' stares sear
bruises into my soul, till wounded tears
spill open as tears flowing from dishonour.

Their rude whispers grow louder,
growling through muffles:
'Hey there, this is my city.
Get the hell outta here.'

I stay quiet, keeping to myself.
My silence is perceived as a threat.
I smile politely to push away their fear,
but it is mistaken as sinister,
like I bear mischievous behaviour.

Their city streets erupt with rioting,
burning and looting their own, claiming,
'It's because of us; they're angry at our presence.
Numbers too many are growing, no space
for their children in schools,
no jobs, we've taken them all.
Yet we're idle, unemployed immigrants,
and me, I'm just studying abroad.'

Awaiting my return to my homeland
where my skin isn't tarnished,
where my name sounds easy,

and strangers smile politely,
unafraid to ask me how my day's been.
And although it isn't heaven,
I never lack hope on hellish days.

Here, the greener pastures harbour snakes,
slithering like jeers hissing from their lips.
The greener pastures are simply mulch,
covering the maggot-infested rot infecting the soils.

Marie Bashford-Synnott

## Writing Life

A book of poems and washing powder,
apple tart and Mendelssohn,
the hoover and my typewriter –
so my life goes on.

Washing floors and planting roses,
the lighthouse and my little son,
children's fights and D.H. Lawrence –
so my life goes on.

Temper tantrums, birthday dresses,
arguments, the silent phone,
*La Bohème* and quiet evenings –
so my life goes on.

A novel with both joy and sorrow,
high romance and battles won,
every page a new tomorrow –
so my life goes on.

Trish Bennett

PORT NA BPÚCAÍ
*The Ghost's Jig*

As the darkness descends before Macnas,
don't stand too close to the Tiger-Mammy
blown-in on the Celtic breeze,
for she has brought her children to see the parade.
She has entitlements. They've been there since three.

Don't say that your husband's people
have been there for three hundred years
or that you've travelled for half a day
so your daughter can see the parade,
for the Tiger-Mammy's Galwegian now.
This gives her the right to insult you *as Gaeilge*.

You've learnt school Irish too, enough
to sell foals at Maam Cross in your youth,
and to understand all she says, but you just smile
and wave. You smile and wave because you know
that the Mammy's about to blow.

Her young, high on Haribo Worms,
race out over the road. She roars
and they leap into their father's arms.
He wrestles one to his shoulder, the other, his hip,
dances a jig as he loses it.

Your daughter – high on her Daddy's shoulders,
gets a smiley-face sticker from a Macnas girl
in a rainbow hat. The crowd surge in a wave
as the darkness lifts with the eerie light from a ghost ship.
A puppet dog at the bow opens his mouth,
reminds you of Judge from *Wanderly Wagon*.

You chew Aunty Nellie's bonbons to the beat of the
drums,
watch a giant bearded druid at the stern of the boat
with pearlescent eyes that blink
as he waves his savage hands.
Black-skulled Púcaí in ashen white robes,
thread so slow, they seem to float
through billowing smoke.

A lighthouse shines across a sea of heads,
dancers shout a rhythmic chant, swing monster gulls
like wands to cast a clearing spell.
When the banshee rises from the mist of her dress,
Tiger-Mammy and family have vanished,
blown out by the gale of Port na bPúcaí.

Claire Blennerhassett

PIVOT

Pivot, to something new and unexpected.
Pivot, aware, from the gauze of the familiar,
and into the mouth of the sun.
Allow to fall the blest
libations of vast skies
to whet the dried-out stonework
of your foundations.
Fall away the rickety scaffold,
the leaning tower of *so much stuff*
that seeks to drag you, unrelenting,
towards a gravity not of your own.

Pull out the binding block,
and rise your essence from its tomb.
Exhale the mould and damp of this
familiar disservice
to your light,
as you ooze and evaporate
through cracks of shoddy wattle
that can no longer hold you.

You, discerning eye of magpie,
starling, crow, you,
the murmuration of effortless fluidity
immense in the wonder of the heavens –
entrust your carrion beak to peck
the worthwhile treasures from old remains,
and nestle them with reverence
in the gleeful sprite of new.

Grow forth the lofty wing,
rooting deep, and branching high,
like the surging pulse of awoken Spring

as it unfurls your chlorophyllic brilliance,
this becoming,
this green fire
of you.

Sara Boyce

### Revelation

In a rented house,
water pours from her ceiling.
She weeps prayers to Allah
while a company man
tells her she'll need a spigot
to measure the water pressure
flowing through her light fittings,
so he can assess how to respond
to her request for help.
All contacts washed away
by the tossed sea crossing,
she feels her life ebb,
slip its flimsy mooring.
Later, in a homeless hostel,
she lingers by the window,
sees runnels of rainwater
dislodge leaves and insects,
nature uprooting itself.
Outside, a sandwich-board man
stands his apocalyptic ground,
Sunday shoes planted
on red, white and blue; implacable
in his black letter call
to *Repent, Repent, Repent.*
To her,
his revelation of fire and floods
of wars, plague and pestilence
is yesterday's news.

Yvonne Boyle

## Catastrophic Loss of Function

'He still has his personality,'
was the first thing my sister said.
'I am there to see you settled in at home
and to listen,' I said.
'And listen to things I am not saying,' she said.

In the church foyer I said:
'Have two sentences ready –
you will be asked questions by many people.'
She said: 'I have prepared something
to say after the service'
and in her hand she had a sheet.

She stood up in church.
She went through all the things
her husband still had:
*breathe         spirit*
*arms* (one stronger than the other)
*hands* (less swollen now)
*eyes      faculties*
*appreciation of visitors.*

The day after, her daughter asked me
'What did she say?
What did she say?'
and I asked my sister
to send her daughters a copy,
for I could not yet repeat her words.

For at the end my sister said:
'Please pray for the surgeon.
He is devastated.

He needs to keep helping people.
Please read this verse with me.
I need your help with it.
*The Lord gives*
*and the Lord takes away.*
*Blessed be the name of the Lord.'*

Caroline Bracken

## Bon Voyage

She had always loved the sea
but wasn't keen on water,
unless it was carbonated,
flavoured with lemon and lime,
so she bought a boat,
installed it in her sitting room.

She had to get rid of the coffee table,
a couch and two armchairs
to make it fit. It wasn't a trawler,
rather a fishing dinghy
with oars, wooden slats for seats
and a hull painted crimson.

She christened it Gráinne Mhaol,
after the Pirate Queen of Mayo,
lined it with bubble wrap
and Ottoman-style cushions,
stuffed with her newly-cut hair
on which she reclined,

a glass of Prosecco in one hand,
carton of Pringles in the other,
set sail for France, Italy, Norway
or wherever the subtitled thriller
on Netflix was located that night,
a search for a woman's body
washed up on some distant shore.

Marie Breen-Smyth

## The Secret of a Long Life

There was never a time when I knew
Without doubt or lingering regret
There was nothing left for me.
I am slow to know when it's time to go.

Without doubt or lingering regret
It took betrayal or hate or lovelessness
I am slow to know when it's time to go.
I must hit the road once more.

It took betrayal or hate or lovelessness
The onslaughts had to tell me
I must hit the road once more.
Life is liveable anywhere but here.

The onslaughts had to tell me
I could do no right
Life is liveable anywhere but here.
Exile is the solution and the problem.

I could do no right
There was nothing left for me.
Exile is the solution and the problem.
There was never a time when I knew.

Clodagh Brennan Harvey

'AND THE WINNER IS ...'

Walking in the park
this mist-heavy morning,
little dogs in tartan coats
brazenly sniffing their pals,
I feel pensive.

It's time to up my game a bit,
take on other issues,
acquire new skills,
have a bigger life, for Christ's sake:
I'm learning to crochet.

I'm starting with hearts,
small, red hearts,
then bigger hearts,
then bigger hearts still.

I'll hide them all over the park –
under stones,
behind trees,
along the trails,
in the coffee shop –
the park will be all a-buzz with it.

It's a simple game:
the one with the biggest heart wins.

Jacquie Burgess

## Call and Response

A blackbird calls his alarm
in the fallen apple tree
alert for danger,
the hidden terrors
the unsafety
of new ground.

Where will he land?
If the old ways are gone,
the nest broken,

my tears shed,
chilled on my cheek
alone with so much loss.

Like my ancient longing
beyond time
carrying the weight of worlds
of many lives
held back by
remembered suffering.

What is that scent?
A note has changed
in the awakening earth.
You can fly, he cries,
you can swoop,
whoop in the sunlight,
in the wild blue yonder.

Come flame of joy,
come playfellow mine
across the wall.

Here are soft landings ...
daisies, plantain,
honey from the hives.

A lost child's yearning,
new-found child laughing,
arms open wide.
Come now sweet thing,
it is soul time.

Lynn Caldwell

## L͏ONELY IS JUST ONE LETTER AWAY FROM LOVELY

so I write that one letter,

fill it with the day's absences,
the night's laments, the stories
I tell myself when I can't sleep,
the ones about the birds that share
their food or the tree that won't stop
giving, how laughter echoes in large
rooms, lilacs can bring you home
and coffee says *welcome, come right in*.

I transcribe the tune that hums along
in fresh morning air, the sunlight
on the table as I write, the sticky stamp
taste on my tongue.
I write your name, your place,
send my heart

in this one letter
to you.

Mary Rose Callaghan

RESUSCITATION

Past midnight and A&E is empty.
The doctor wears a hijab, is under five feet.
Too young to be in charge, I think.
'You wish resuscitation?' she asks.

'I'd like a cup of tea, please.'
My brother speaks from a trolley,
hooked to several monitors.
Hair grey-blond, eyes a brilliant blue,
and all the good looks in the family.

The doctor repeats her question.
I beckon her out to the corridor.
'Please don't use that word.'
She looks at me blankly. 'Which word?'
I tower over her. *'Resuscitation.'*
'But there's a clot? He's 65.'
'I don't want him frightened.'
The porter wheels him to the lift.
I take stairs to the empty ward.

'Don't they have any tea?' he moans.
None in the machine, so I bring coffee.
He sips in bed. 'How long till Christmas?'
But it's only the Feast of All Souls.
'I want a raincoat, if you can manage.'
I nod. 'We'll make a list.'

'How are you feeling now?' I ask.
'Can't they spare some tea?'
It arrives with toast and cheese.
'No tomatoes,' he sighs, 'a pity.'

'Your appetite's a good sign.'
'But I can't eat toast!'

At dawn a reprieve: there's no clot.
My brother's always high on hope.
'A pity we missed Halloween!'
I doze in a chair. 'There'll be another day.'
'How many to my birthday?'
'I'm too tired to count.'
'Any chance of more tea?'

I'm at the door when he calls again.
'You know the raincoat? The green shiny sort.
And get the tree tomorrow!
And lights! They'll all be gone!
A crib too! *Please!*'
Down the corridor, I hear him singing
that hymn about the manger.

Opposite the car park, a shop's already lit.
A plastic angel winks giddily,
promising hope to all. And happiness.
When my brother was born, I was nine.
He was my baby, then,
the only one I ever had.

Marion Clarke

SLOWING DOWN

I bump into him that morning as the bell is still tolling for half ten mass. As usual I am running late, enroute to my office in the nearby nursery school.

As dapper as always, Dad wears his three-quarter length trench coat and tweed cap. I watch him cross Queen Street and step cautiously onto the newly-laid pavement – so slippery when wet that the whole town has been complaining about it. He smiles when he looks up and realises it's me. I wait, take his arm and walk alongside him. Together we progress along the green railings of the park until we turn into Great George's Street, his blackthorn stick clicking off the flagstones. It sounds brisk enough to me, but he stops and says, 'Ah, you go on ahead to work. love, I can't keep up with you anymore. I'll only hold you back.' This is the first time I will shed a silent tear for him.

deep winter ...
Dad's garden swing seat
still creaking

Susan Condon

## First Dance

Across the room
I see you.
Your slate grey eyes
meet mine.
My breath stops.
Mesmerised, I can but stare,
unable to break away
from your silent gaze.
I wait,
until you
move your head,
not wanting
to be the first
to break the spell,
terrified
you might never
*see* me again.
Lights dim.
You appear at my side,
whisper in my ear
with a warm breath.
I nod,
allow you
to take my hand.
You lead me
to the centre
of the dance floor.
A song,
about the air tonight,
plays on and on,
the drum beat
pounding like my heart.

We sway,
in unison, bodies
entwined in the darkness.

Martina Dalton

TO RAISE A WRITING ROOM

More easily than I had bargained for,
the tree surgeon appeared – the uneasy shift
of his boots. Wondered

if I'd thought it through.
The scrape of tree against the sky, holding up
the whole world.

The machine that would not quit, to turn it all
to dust. The heavy limbs I asked to leave,
that I might later make a bowl

or a chair or a child's wooden cart –
isn't that what I'm supposed to do?
With every splinter that I write.

The burning thing: the twenty or so years it took
to grow, to carve its place. Ten leaves of flame
detached, now dimming in the light.

I forgot to tell the blackbird. All I have left –
is his blackbird song. How he responded
note for note when I summoned him:

the recording on my phone. How I worried
afterwards if I'd tricked him, pretending
I am someone I am not.

How I'll have to use it again, come spring –
to bring him back. Nail a perch of wood
to the felt.

And the blackbird too will have to gather
from that gape: build anew a sacred place
high up – to hone and hold its song.

Maureen Daly

BE COURAGEOUS

You lying in bed with
sexless cancer and me,
your innings nearly up.
You liked the words 'innings'
and 'declare to ashes.'
You said 'marry again.'

I remember when the one flight a week to Corsica
with our honeymoon luggage onboard
left us behind at Heathrow.
We triumphed, arriving two days later.

We honeymooned at home for two years,
drinking fresh elderflower wine in the summer.
Fizzy, made us dizzy, I conceived.

I remember you pruned the roses,
listened to Beethoven's 'Les Adieux',
tasted the beef curry; dashed to work
to check prevailing winds, anti-cyclones,
conditions, isobars, gave the weather forecast,
crossing your fingers it would not be worse.

You had a dream to be a Monsieur,
standing to attention to La Marseillaise ...
I flew to Nice three months after your funeral,
dined on niçoise salad,
lapin and crème caramel,
swilled down with rosé wine.
I paid *l'addition* and flew home.

June now the erotic buds of the roses are blooming.

Sorcha de Brún

## Rialacha Cogaidh

Fuair sibh réidh le rialacha an chogaidh agus a gcuid oird
   agus eagair inné,
Nuair a thosaigh na buamaí ag titim agus na pléascáin ag
   screadaíl i lár an lae.
Níl aon áit do rialacha nuair a bhuaileann uaillmhian is
   fonn,
is tá m'áit dhúchais marbh:
Shleamhnaigh gach rud a bhí im sheilbh agam uaim nuair
   a rinne sibh íogán.

Inniu a chuirim i leataobh an aimsir chaite go deo agus
   choíche,
i gcroílár na hoíche nuair a bhíonn na heitleáin mhíleata ag
   déanamh a ndíchill,
ag síneadh is ag sní trí spéartha liatha ócair os mo chionn,
tá mo mhuintir ag teitheadh:
Stuálaim paca ag cur thar maoil lem shaol mar a bhíodh,
   'is bailím liom.

Gach lá adhlacaim m'aimsir fháistineach le mo leanbh
   thíos sa chré,
feicim m'iníon lena fiche bliain d'uafás, mo mhac, an t-
   oileánach ina dheireadh ré.
Tá Parlaimintí na mBan, na bPáistí agus na bhFear sa
   stráice tite,
is m'fhear céile ag caoineadh le léire:
An Bhréige Chlasaiceach i réim agus logainmneacha na
   dúthaí tréigthe.

Ach fiafraíonn tú an bhfuil na rialacha á gcur i bhfeidhm in
 ainneoin an réabtha,
rialacha a athraíonn de réir mar a oireann daoibhse, lucht
 na nua-chléire.
Agus nuair a deir tú liom go bhfuilim ag cliseadh i
 ndomhan úr seo na bruíne,
éiríonn ceisteanna amach ina dtonnta:
Cathain a imreofar an cluiche cogaidh leis na rialacha
 céanna imeartha?

Helen Dempsey

## JANE DONNELLY

If I found you
I would visit your orange grave
outside of marching season.

Is it marked, or has grass levelled the plot?
I want to see for myself
if your name is carved in stone.

I would lay flowers over you and pray,
tell you how brave I think you were,
make the Sign of the Cross, recite Hail Marys.

Then I would make my way to the workhouse
where you lived, and alone
delivered my grandfather.

An official registered the birth.
I see his sloping hand but not yours,
nor your mark, nor a father's name.

Your surname was misspelt in the census.
All those lies repeated to two generations,
yet I long to visit your home place

where kerbs are stained union
with an aversion to green,
where *aves* are not appreciated.

But would you be ashamed of me?

Doreen Duffy

## Things are Getting Ready to Happen
*after Eavan Boland,* In a Time of Violence, *1994*

This main street
divided north and south
by games and childish rhymes

fruit flies make my kitchen
their banquet hall
floaters before my eyes

impossible to grasp
a blue-sky laundered sheet
left out to rot
dotted with mould

a million satellites
circle the earth
the moon
hauls the tide

China blue water pools
yellow lights
quadrant and boundary lines

a broken bottle
its message
swallowed in nets
caught in waves

from the inside out
fruit flies feed
out of sight

Ger Duffy

## Teratogen

Let's start with my father standing in the back garden
under a gibbous moon,
searching the sky for a Russian Sputnik,
his eyes on the half-moon,
his mind in the bedroom
where my mother is giving birth.
The doctor ushers the nurse to the bathroom with the
baby.
Let's stop before my father must be sedated,
before my mother learns her baby has no arms.
Maybe nobody gets ruined.
My father works eighteen-hour days for twenty years.
My mother's best friend is her bag of pills.
I'll rewrite this whole scene and this time Chemie-
Grunenthal will do the tests properly,
my sister will get to have arms
and when I am born
there will be so much joy
you won't believe it.

You won't believe it,
my sister will get to have arms
and when I am born
there will be so much joy.
I'll rewrite this whole scene and this time Chemie-
Grunenthal will do the tests properly.
Maybe we're ok and my mother won't need
her bag of pills.
Maybe my father comes home
and nobody gets ruined.
Maybe my mother learns her baby is a girl,
and when the doctor hands my sister to my father,

he is congratulated.
Maybe he does see a Russian Sputnik,
while his mind is in the bedroom
as my mother is giving birth
as he stands in the back garden
under a gibbous moon.

Catherine Dunne

OLD PHOTOGRAPHS

I like best the ones of sepia-fleshed fathers,
freeze-framed forever in the vastness of suit lapels
and buttoned, belted overcoats.

Your right hand streaks a white blur
across the grainy surface as you
flick the ash from your constant Gold Flake.

Laughing into camera, your comment, faded now,
falls in ripples among The Pals.
One gives a mock salute, captures your attention

and affection, lasting fully fifty years through
the murky tones of forgotten photographs.
Later, the tones are clearer:

Black and white in the album of your life.
Post-war austerity makes trousers slimmer,
dresses shorter.

Velvet bows on her bridal gown, sewn by sisters
weaving close the fabric of their lives.
Then and always pulled tight, tighter

by a common thread of steel.
Babies play with buckets of potatoes in summer sunshine.
A dog rolls on garden soil unsoftened yet by grass or age.

My mother smiles into sunshine.
She sits in the green and red-striped deckchair:
It smells of winter storage in the garden shed

among the jars and bottles that soon become
the magic currency of shop.
The gentle twenty years

filled with happy lack of order
and baby souvenirs.
The same back garden, green

and brightly tended, fills now with our shrill children.
Birthdays, anniversaries, cakes being cut –
everything recorded,

waiting to be ordered, lying in
the blue and battered cardboard box.
I need no camera now, to capture

final images of an illness.
No sepia tones to soften
the stark and breathless suffering.

Our family divided and united
by the garishness of grief.
My life before unchanged

by mourning,
awakened now
to the colour, shape and form

of my own mortality.

Micheline Egan

## Not Linear or Elegant

The poor divil lost oxygen
on her arrival down the birth canal
that Christmas Day in 1961
and again, on her last day
at twenty minutes past teatime.

I mark the moment on the butcher's calendar.
I prune and pull
two serviceable black dresses
and a good coat from the wardrobe.
I invest in 80 Barry's teabags.
I turn the heat on full blast.

After her funeral mass
I avoid the cemetery.
I cannot let that harsh bromide burn into me.

I want to remember her
in her own home
with the radio dial on 2FM
wrapped in 24/7 waking care,
the range lit, the telly on,
the mugs of tea served up.

Afterwards, I take her polka dot duvet cover,
sleep under it for weeks,
keep her roll-on deodorant
only ever administered by the carers who showered her.

The wise young GP with Leitrim in her
said *don't be joining grief counselling groups
for at least six months to a calendar year.*

Allow the heartbreak to ambush you,
it's not linear or elegant,
it does not distinguish the gender of who witnesses it.
Prepare for clumsy
prepare for shock
and be careful about who's listening,
you do not want their
competitive grief
as you search the world for balm
to soften your sandblasted heart.

There will be lots of days.
Lots
where you're not fit to be out,
where vexatious people will rattle your coordinates.

Attracta Fahy

OPPOSING OPPOSITES

I dream of my mother,
at the kitchen table,
smiling.
She has returned
from behind that far hill.
We make bread,
we don't speak,
language is a blood soaked weapon.

She's making signs –
*others will have you believe*
*opposing opposites,*
*you cannot bomb your way into peace,*
*there are children dying*
*for no other reason*
*than they were born,*
*children forced to fight*
*who will never know who won,*
*or if the war ended.*

I wake to reality. My mother is dead.
Oh come back, mother,
I've been spellbound
by dreams,
clouds heavy with ash.

Mother is not coming back.
The children are not coming back.
Only the dead know peace.

Helen Fallon

SIERRA LEONE SATURDAYS

Weekends, I walk the pink path to Freetown,
wave to women wading in water pools,
whacking clothes on rocks, babies on their backs.
The market sellers call from stalls heaving
scarlet chillies, plump purple aubergines,
and shiny green clumps of cassava leaves.
Long-fingered Mandingo traders unpack
bales of cloth from tin trunks. The sun dances
on swirling shades of blue, red and yellow.
I join the others in the bakery.
We sip thick coffee, share stories – our posts,
places we plan to visit, news from home.

All that was long ago. Things changed, war came,
I changed too. Now I sip milky coffee
in Costa, watch the feeble sun fade, sky darken
and rain weep down the window pane.

Carole Farnan

## Seven Different Ways of Looking at Poets
*after Wallace Stevens*

i

Thought collectors:
first netting, then bringing to earth
before pinning them on velvet.

ii

Night explorers:
shining Davy-lamps ahead;
treading darkness, embracing it.

iii

Pan-handlers:
rootling in streams, through gravel and dirt,
chasing that elusive gleam.

iv

Magpie linguists:
pecking at dialects,
stealing the shiny words.

v

Griots and minstrels:
plucking tunes, familiar and new
for any listener, or none.

vi

Word-weavers:
turning the everyday into comforters
or ornate tapestries.

vii

Sonneteers and balladeers,
rhymesters and rappers,
versifiers and mystifiers.
Poets.

Tanya Farrelly

PAINTING MY GRANDMOTHER'S NAILS
*i.m. Jean Cleary*

I paint my grandmother's nails,
fingers outstretched on my palm,
as lacquer covers lines of age,
transforming parchment hues
to the pearlescence of her youth.

Deirdre Flaherty Brady

## Elegy to my Literary Foremothers[1]

Why call me from afar
when you should be
frolicking in the arts?
Why prod me
to go and do your will –
bring forth your iridescent thoughts
to this unyielding world,
carry on my back your deeds and words?
What know I of your ilk
or the imagination of your times?
If I take up the staff – is it mine?
"Hope rises from the mud"[2]
voices echo in the dark blue air
bubbling iridescently in my mind,
your thoughts and mine intertwined.
A flicker like a Proustian slight
suddenly ignites.
It is I who calls you.

1  Dedicated to the women writers of the Irish Women Writers' Club (1933–1958).
2  Quotation from Blanaid Salkeld's poem, 'No Dream', from her collection, *Hello Eternity* (Elkin Mathews, 1933). This collection won the first 'Book of the Year' literary prize awarded by the Irish Women Writers' Club in 1934.

Bernadette Fox

## The Everyday Fantastic

Soiled, wet, smelling of urea,
plunged into a bucket of sterilising fluid
then boil washed, till all traces
of stain are gone.

A square cloth of terry towel,
plush white, cloud soft,
better by far than a plastic Pampers nappy,
better for baby's tender skin.

But oh, the scrubbing,
steeping, pegging;
fingers raw and chafed,
scalded like a baby's bottom.

An artist sketched the sight:
a line of billowing shapes,
snow-white cloth nappies,
a celebration of the everyday.

I, on the other hand
saw only drudgery.

*(Anne Yeats Exhibition, National Gallery of Ireland)*

Amy Gaffney

## The Breaking Point of a Writer, or Imposter Syndrome

I think I'm becoming more
and more ...
odd.

It's the all-the-time thinking,
I think.
It's so insular.

I look outside,
sometimes,
to watch and think.

I think I can't
mingle with others.
I keep thinking about what they're not saying.

There's the space
that thinking requires.
It gets in the way a little.

It's a wedge,
invisible,
right there in the way.

Odd.
Someone said that about me once,
I think they're right.

I don't feel
odd,
well, not always.

I think it's a *real thing*.
It holds hands
with me. Oddness.

I think that,
I can see it sometimes,
even though it's invisible.

I think, I find,
I'm losing words.
Odd.

Shauna Gilligan

I Left my Womb in Napoli

I could say it fell like cherries,
or rose petals, or
that I bled like a pig.
I could say my swollen belly
was full of air, or jadedness.

But simply put, I bled my way
along once-no-go-Maradona
-muralled-streets overflowing
with the bitter sweetness of
*Limonata a Cosce Aperte.*

Then an old man fell in on
me crouched over a toilet and
I raised my bloodied hands,
hissed *occupata* as clots
tumbled brightly into the
bowels of *centro storico.*

In Napoli people leave hearts,
or wallets, or never let them go.
I left my womb pulsating
in the catacombs, beneath sea water
lapping at the lips of
crumbling colourful high rises.
A womb as lucky and
as red as the *curniciello.*

Aimee Godfrey

I̲n̲ W̲hich my G̲randfather is P̲layed by E̲ugene L̲evy

We used to do this every year,
but this year, after everything,
these stacks of photographs
are more important
than they have ever been.

A film in dual tone freeze frame,
a silver screen love story
I couldn't write if I tried,
through time and tide and moon phase,
until we can orient ourselves in their cinematic orbit
by the colour of his eyebrows.

We make them our memories too,
so that we can take them with us when we go.
So that we are never too far from home.

Anita Gracey

## Aunt Beatrice

Aunt Beatrice blew into my family on angel dust. She spreads joy wherever she goes. She is party hats, picnic spreads, sticky jam and butterfly buns. If she had wings they'd flitter, with confetti frolicking in the sunlight. I sit on her skirt of rustling meadows, bury in her hair of sugar-sweet clouds, curls wax crescent moons, and intoxicate on her singsong calm. She glides from her stone-cut house, low-lit paraffin lamps, windows warp to the floor and board games held up the ceiling. Horses trot to nuzzle her, blue tits dazzle with acrobatics and spring wells sing. Dogs don't bark, nettles won't sting and bees only buzz. The worst I could say of Aunt Beatrice is my cheeks ache after seeing her – still echoing the laughter of harps.

In storybook charm
true heroines don't wear capes –
a happy ever.

Angela Graham

## Do Unto Others

I will roll up my net and sheathe my knife
– I've seen in dreams how heavily your life
weighs down on mine and I allow it to.
Yours is the face that all my tyrants wear,
about to turn its dreadful gaze on me,
you minotaur. But *this* dream brought the key:
your puzzled tears – you trap me in your lair
for company! You ... are in prison too.
I will call off my spoilers and un-snare
the stream. Un-coiling slick weed anklets spun
to pull you down, I'll reel my shadows in.
I am my gorgon. I must meet my stare
and live, then turn and meet you eye to eye,
un-armed, alert, eager for your reply.

Mim Greene

## Doorway
*for Angela*

The remembering of that holy place
where we knitted words together,
where I sat at your feet,
and 'talk it mama'.

Where you listened to my child brain and eked it forward,
closer than ever before,
touching a place of crystal clarity
and oceans deep.

Thank you for those poetry times.
You gave me a gift
that is saving my life.

All is forgiven.
I see your pain,
and I know you see mine.

We have knitted our wounds together,
our pain now has meaning.

The secret code of mother and daughter.

A door is now open
for the brave to walk through.
I take your hand.

Anita Greg

## The Mayday Wyrtsong
*If I was a plant I'd be a wyrt*

purple tinted, appearing after showers
pungent, fumigant with tiny flowers

I cure dropsy, mopsy, cottontail and fever
I cure ipso facto
lorem ipsum dolor
vikay versa and on the dot.
I cure them on a Maunday, a Tirsday,
a Mercredi, a Thorsday
a Friggesday, a Saturnday but niver on the Sabbathday
for that's nae right

> "Oh where ha'e ye been, Lord Randall my son?
> Oh where ha'e ye been, my blue eyed one?"
> "In the woods dear mother, the wyld woods dear mother
> Oh make my bed quick cos I'm gonna be sick and I fain would
> lay doon an die"

I cure sweet itch in horses
ticks and louses, lift off curses

> *way down the bank where the wyld wyrt grows*
> *among the cresses and the rushy river flows,*
> *all uptangled with the yellow hair of Clementine*
> *tripped and fell into the water, floating in the foamy brine*

I cure drownings, bleedings that will not stop
I cure shingles, strangles and yellow snot
weans too late and weans too soon
the sweating sickness
and the blinding of the moon

"Oh what ate you in yon woods, Lord Randall my son?
Oh what ate you in yon woods, my blue eyed one?"
"I ate wyrts dear mother, wyrts dear mother
Oh make my bed quick cos I'm gonna be sick and I fain would
lay doon an die"

You'll find me in dark places in among the grasses
nettles docks and ferny fronds
down among the roots in stagnant ponds
I cure leprosy, rhapsody and bloody flux
hysteria, wisteria, diptheria and pox
aphids, youphids
and blight in ducks.

Sinéad Griffin

## The Phillumenist

Matchboxes, lucifers, cardboard matchbook combs,
these she keeps in a crystal bowl,
though she herself never smoked.

She has salvaged them from his trouser pockets,
mementos of places he frequents,
the cover pictures interest her,

salons, white-apron waiters, gilded mirrors,
like an archive of where he eats dinner,
the thin of a Cigarillo on his lips.

While at home she stockpiles her fire.
You never know when you might need a strike,
never know when the power might go out.

Sharon Guard

## The Middle Age

It starts: a suddenly clicking knee,
striations ominous on a lip,
pucks, rosy cheeks, nostril hairs,
lines in unfeasible directions,
hair-like-wire or wire-like-hair shoots
from recently smooth skin, hoary
wrinkled crone claws on display.
You're never that age! they say, polite
acts of judgement, and you accept
blame with dyes, fillers, creams and
threads, pumping poison in your head,
believe the conceit of youth in tragic
abundance, crave relevance;
apologetic, embarrassed,
as if for a bad choice, unintended
consequence, social faux pas, but!
It can no longer be circumvented ...
contemporaries betray you, shuffle
off too soon: the bell curve begins.

Christine Hammond

## Flight Path

Long and languid
the humid nights hang
heavy as a cloak
festooned by Ursa Major

in the lane bats squeak, cats screech
a river runs tidal
and the moon's soft filament flickers
dying to sunrise

slowly, the wild geese appear
a prelude of eager starts, then
more and more
join to shape the sacred apex

faith in formation
divine travellers lining the sky
calling their sojourn across the dawn
gifting light from a slipstream

Rachel Handley

## THEY

When I tell you who I am
you tell me that I am wrong.
As if my born blood speaks words
to you that it refuses me.
As if my years, whispering only to you,
filled me up, pink, and ready
to be pressed into your shape.
But blood is made in the mouth,
my whole heart sang to get it there,
to flush out the stones you grew.

Phyl Herbert

OUTBURST

Run ... run ... run ...
the church our playground,
we fill our young mouths
with cold water from outside taps.
The dare – TO HOLD IT IN –
'first to the post wins the race.'

Run ... run ... run ...
no time to genuflect.
Sprays of water glisten on altar rails.
The age of reason
yet to come.

Run ... run ... run ...
the church your playground no more.
In the dark of the confession box
the priest's voice roars
a mortal sin on your soul

Run ... run ... run ...
you wear the tag of *damaged goods*
dance away the rock and roll years
in dizzy lights and sexy nights
then tumble down when the music stops.

Run ... run ... run ...
across the water with your shame and your lies
to a place where girls such as you can hide
your story held close for decades until
the fruit of that sin comes into sight.

Run ... run ... run ...
back to where you started from
a blank sheet that must be written on.

The dam of silence bursts,
you are seven again and running
'first to the post wins the race.'
You spill out your secret to the media altar.
A story, your story,
that could no longer
– BE HELD IN.

Florence Heyhoe

## In Good Spirits

Folded sheets, anchored to the railings, with masks for faces, flap about the garden of the lodge where we are staying. The mirrors are fogged with cobwebs where giant spiders lurk ... red eyed and hairy legged. A tall man with a tarantula on his head is chatting to a small man peeping out from under a pork-pie hat. Someone says to my husband, 'this is an old folks' home; we have all murdered our wives!'

We hear music in the afternoon, music in the evening as we eat our dinner, and at five o'clock in the morning as they stagger back to rooms adjacent to ours singing, 'dirty old town, dirty old town.'

As I head for my last breakfast I notice the door to room ten is ajar. Inside a man in a green football shirt sleeps in a chair, his head on his chest. After breakfast, he is still asleep.

all night long
the rhythm
of rattling bones

Jennifer Horgan

## BODY

We write it – and our words make flesh.
Our scarred, wet, trembling hair on bone
is birthed, the months left curled in our lives
like frigid rope, unfurl. We roar our breasts,
sore and heavy with milk, our stained mattresses,
our mess. We bleed through vowels, our hands
pawing nouns like inflamed gum. We paste skin
across every rhythm, sway lines like hips, blaze
our shapes in libraries and bookshops. Recite
poems about labia and HRT. We, who are made
of welt and broken surfaces, leak our bodies
in assonance. Scream, until we are trapped
inside half-dying shells again, no longer trapped
in beds, kitchens, in laundries, in prisons.
Not in asylums, or in convents, but in our own
poems. We are so thinly sliced again, while men
sit and watch from the grey aisles of intellect
nodding, blind to their ceaseless spill.

Sacha Hutchinson

## 1980 TO 1986
*after Hugo Williams*

Now that I have forgotten
the Royal College of Surgeons,
now that I can't remember
York Street and its tenements,
St Stephen's Green in early light,
the mallards in dirty ponds,
the locker room where I was
too shy to look at you.

Now that I have forgotten
our escapes to Bewley's,
its Harry Clarke windows,
cherry buns and strong coffee,
the hours in the anatomy laboratory
with the formaldehyde smell
of half-dissected bodies,
the five muscles that inserted
into the greater trochanter,
never remembering piriformis.

Now that I've forgotten the smog
that curved along the corridors,
the old library, my head heavy
with signs, symptoms, differentials
so it would rest on medical books,
smell paper, page, words,
sleep for minutes, then lift
to cram for the next exam.

I feel sure nothing remains of that time
but this yearbook full of young faces.
I remember where everyone sat

in those lofty, lecture theatres
but would struggle now
with most of the names.

Jean James

I WAS SMALL

In Fermanagh
I hid from my brother and sister,
an old game we loved to play.
It was late summer;
shadows sliced through gaps
in the birch trees
down to the loam floor,
a bed of stealthy sponge.

I was still,
they would never find me.
I was safe
in a green womb of bracken
and an ocean of ferns,
tendrils curling over me,
fingers squirrelled into earth
where treasures rested.

Once I found a copper coin
with a wren on it,
and a fragment of pottery,
fragile Beleek, and I thought
of folk who once lived here
before the bog grew stronger.
Was it their voices I could hear,
or something else?

My brother told me stories
of how even giant men
were swallowed up
in black holes and never seen again.
I was small

but said to myself that here
inside this green church
I was safe.

For why would I not be
I said to my seven-year-old self
as a whip of wind
rustled the leaves above me.
I felt myself shrinking
like a seed into the ground,
dumb, dark, damp.

More voices
and someone said, 'Found.'

Rosemary Jenkinson

## Heliophile

All her life, my mother lapped at the sun,
sucked its honey up through a straw,
her arms outstretched like a hieratic worshipper,
chin tilted, eyes closed under its drowsing celestial power,
and she would drift for hours on her sun lounger,
drenching her skin in Ambre Solaire,
tutting at my pallor, casting a withering
roll of her brown eyes at how my skin lobstered
and peeled in calamine calamity,
while the sunlight coated her in an even golden glow.
To see her, you'd have thought our lawn
was the Côte d'Azur,
the sound of traffic, the whisper of the sea.

On the Twelfth she would stay there,
unmoved, looking at the insides of her orange eyelids,
and when a bomb purred deep in the city
her lashes would tremble but never open.
Then, as the sun set, she would stand, snap her bikini
back over her buttocks
and slink loose-limbed into the kitchen
in voluptuous self-appreciation.

Sometimes she'd tell the story of her glory days:
how at twenty years old she holidayed in Italy
where the *regazzi* were fooled by her olive hues
into thinking she was Italian too –
*Bella, bella!* went their cries
when she sashayed through the *piazza*.

But now, in her last months of lung cancer
and on the best day of the year,

she hirples out to the garden,
scapula hunched, her wheezing breaths
in tune with the wind's rustle of the leaves.
I attend to her with cushions,
placing them on the wooden bench like some courtier
while she has her audience with the sun,
her shirt cuffs swamping her hands, white hat
wielding a swaddling shadow over her face,
mindful of the danger of the light on her chemo,
but how I long for her to feel the sun on her skin
one last time,
so what I do is stay with her,
roll up my sleeves,
exposing my white skin
to the naked glare
and take the rays on her behalf,
burning, scorching, reddening by the second,
immolating myself on the patio pyre,
making sure to tell her
how beautiful it feels.

Cath-Ann Kavanagh

## Silent Treatment

Land your cruel words on me
shout your vitriol from the rooftops
sneer those familiar lips in scorn
shrug, furrow, blank me, glare
roll your eyes in pretend despair
*but in the weight of your silence, I'm forlorn.*

Deliver me loud rock and heavy metal noise
practise your violin or trombone wildly
bang the upstairs doors with menace
clatter spiked muddy boots in the hall
clench both fists for the forthcoming brawl
*but in the weight of your silence, I'm forlorn.*

Cut your creative wisecracks on me
deride me for my naïve stupidity
mock me in the presence of your allies
seek support with that winning grin
from those who consider you the kingpin
*but in the weight of your silence, I'm forlorn.*

Hannah Kiely

## SHE, BRAVER THAN I

I write you into my poems
as I live in my world, now

me Virginia, you my Vita
me Elizabeth, you my Lota

like words on a page to the non-poet
you slip past in their meaning

I made that choice, then
I can't go back, I grieve for what

we started at the ocean, when we
laid bare our salted skin to the world

the sea has always drawn me
under many moons and galaxies

I watch the same moon as you now
from a different place

how we loved then, I think of you
as I listen to *The Power of Love* on repeat

you knew what you wanted
so did I, but you, dearest creature

you were so much braver than I
you, the one that got away

Thérèse Kieran

## TO A POET
*on reading Jane Hirshfield*

Thank you for showing me that I already have everything
I need: a lamp, pen and paper; a desk to be busy at
scratching words into the blank page over and over.

Thank you for helping me to name
what I have become without my telling everyone.
I have let go, so I can become more of myself.

Thank you, for by your quiet insistence I have time
and silence to make poems that weigh almost nothing,
yet they persist in accompanying me as I go my own way.

Bethan Kilfoil

DEFIBRILLATOR

it's in a box attached to a grey stone wall
on the mountain road that passes Bryn Awel
the house my Taid built a hundred years ago
between fields of bracken and sheep
spread over heather hills under tumbling clouds
where we played and ran down to the farm below

put there I suppose in case of emergency
a lost and breathless hiker maybe
tourists out for a weekend drive
disorientated by wilderness and warp of time

but in truth I can't imagine who'll ever need it:
a memory, sudden whip of wind, shaft of sunlight
blackbird song, a primrose astonished as a star –
surely these are enough to jolt the heart

*trans:*
*Bryn Awel/Breeze Hill*
*Taid/Grandfather*

Susan Knight

VISIONS OF A THIEF OF NIGHT

A sudden darkness as the power fails.
I am alone, out of the city, in a quiet place,
a house among the hills, that's tossed and twirled
on waves of wind, deep waters of the night.

These are uncharted seas and I'm no sailor girl,
crouched by the log fire, peering at the embers
to fix the little bit of light that anchors me in place.
A branch flares up and shadows shape
the room I used to see,
now grand, grotesque and tremulous.
It glimmers down to that same rolling
in the head, that tilting at the base of all.

And now I'm drawn into the red
heart of the fire. If that is hell
then why's my father smoking placidly his pipe?
It flares and fades and flares again.
A swan-necked woman near him and a hag,
that man who served the beer, old whatshisname.
A hundred faces, all undone by death
or so it seems. And then I turn to see

a brilliance lighting up the room.
Familiar furniture takes back its form,
a couch, an armchair and a coffee table.
The moon is out, then, and I run
to pull the curtains back.
But clouds are hanging low and lour.
No moon, no stars, no help in that direction.
It can't be dawn unless the night
forgot itself and left too soon

a victim of enchantment.
So what? I see the falling fields, the mountains
over them like breakers in a storm
and all as clear as day. While in the room
the cup and glass, the shells, the pebbles
and the bone-white wood. Flotsam
and jetsam of a life grown old.

I see them all as cast upon a reef
for I've been granted the night vision of a thief.

Donna Leamy

## THALASSOPHILE

As sure as a wave returns to the sea
when the sun and the moon pull the tide,
you too have come to depend on me.

'I don't need a programme – you wait and see.'
I'm supportive, I'm at your side,
but as sure as a wave returns to the sea,

can I believe the words uttered to me,
considering the extent of your lies?
I fear you'll return to dependency.

'It's different this time,' you declare to me,
with conviction that can't be denied,
but as sure as a wave returns to the sea,

and how convincing you can be,
I sense a change of the tide.
My fear you'll return to dependency,

no longer a hunch but a guarantee,
when I discover the bottles you hide.
And as sure as a wave returns to the sea,
you too have returned to dependency.

Róisín Leggett Bohan

## THE PATH

That day of the accident, you carried me down this path
running, begging, calling *Oh Jesus no, Jesus no.*
My half-conscious cry was as much for the earth scent
of your neck and my new boots in the hedge,
as for the bicycle wheel and car bumper.

Up the gravel path, beyond the gate
where we used to swing
on the buckled bend of its lower frame,
I navigate the weight
of you, past the spot where I took my first bicycle ride,
earned my bloodied pebbledash knees,
your hand on my shoulder lending belief.

We carry you up the path, a weighted symmetry
between six siblings
and me, to where the solemn pallbearers stand.
Do they practise that look?
I cannot let you down, until I hear your voice,
clear as the stones
beneath my feet – *You can let me go now.*

Nearing your leaving, you called out for me.
I gathered my infant son from his cot,
laid him down on your bed.
*Lift me,* you asked. My arms under yours,
cradling the soapy-scent
of your neck, I carried you to the window
– we watched light lisp the path
over my son's wispy breaths.

Mary Lockhart

## Poetry in Motion

Hands poised over a stainless steel bowl,
after dipping the paws into two flours,
a sprinkle of salt added to the mix.
Your thumb rubbed out hardened bread soda
in your left palm.

That squat jug held the wet ingredient.
A crust had formed on the top
but you swirled a knife through it
to make a consistent liquid,
then made a well and added it to the mix.

Capable hands formed the dough
into a soft pillow with no cracks.
No talk, just kneading gently
all within minutes.
And they were precious.

Consigned to the blackened tin
you flattened gently.
You knew the shape.
A cross to bake evenly
all made by your deft hand.

Shunted into the oven you made
your way for daily mass.
Steps tip-tapping down the hall,
rosary in your right pocket
and a prayer for all on your lips.

Jackie Lynam

GLASS OF POISON

They keep giving her
a glass of *poison* to drink.
Meanwhile Lisa has absconded
from St Joseph's Ward.

*Listen to me, Lisa,*
*you tell the taxi driver to take you straight back.*
*Listen to me, Lisa,*
*if you don't come back we'll have to call the guards.*
*Listen to me, Lisa,*
*your mother is up to high doh.*

Meanwhile Mam's arms are purple
from elbow to wrist.
A thread of blueberry bruises showcasing
the nurses' difficulty in locating a vein.

But today she has makeup on.
*I even put my earrings in,*
she tells me over the phone.
*You have to make an effort,* she says
*otherwise you'd go to seed.*

The hospital stay has scarred her.
Her energy levels are low,
her optimism dimmed.
But she insists on cooking her own meals,
allows us to check in, but not stay over.

*I'm never going into hospital again,* she swears.
*I'd rather stay home and die in my own bed.*
I wonder if Lisa felt the same.

Carmel Lynch

## The Embrace

I watch your head on the pillow, your black hair matted with sweat on this warm summer's evening. You are very tired, you've kicked up a fuss, "No, Grandma" you insisted, Brahms' lullaby was too sedate. You preferred the flickering pics, the colour and movement of other nursery rhymes.

I give in, you move closer, you're exhausted, you try to get comfortable, one hand under your chin and the other one in mine. You fix your little bottom in position as I watch your face scrunch up intensely. How much I love you, little man, is all I can think about, how you've enriched my whole life since the day you were born.

Soon they will have gathered all their data and they'll sift it, categorise it, and put a name on your condition. But I want to tell you it will change nothing as I will always know and love you just exactly as you are.

Your eyelids droop, your breathing grows heavier, your fat little fingers are now curled tightly around mine. You are sleeping peacefully beside me and my heart is full.

It has to be thus. I know you have to go into the system as sure as any child must start school. Your beloved mam has quietly opened doors, is beating down some more, putting all the supports in place so you can know and dance and play and feel and laugh like all the others, just in your own unique way.

I hold you close, you're sound asleep, I'm wide awake as I drink the peace and watch my little buddy so relaxed. I want to stay like this forever.

Tomorrow will come too soon.

Noelle Lynskey

## The Voice Keeper

For twenty years and more,
her room on the mall echoes
with the timbre of boy sopranos,
in rows of promise beside her piano.

She is the moon on the tide of their breath
drawing the faltering airs, holding
each phrase with care until she
shapes their whisper
into song,

into tunes that are swept
along the streetscape
up to the high steeple,
warbles that pipe their way
to the row of horsechestnuts
in their standing ovation
to the keeper who knows the rise
and fall of every phase,
its waxing and waning
like a traditional slow air.

Siobhán Mac Mahon

PAVING THE WAY
*in memory of Eavan Boland 1944–2020*

There is a woman in a country
that is not her own
weeping at a kitchen table,

listening to the radio
as the voices of a nation
celebrate the words of a poet

who has died.
Who wrote, it seems
of a life not unlike her own:

Of the quiet hours
in the dark of a night
feeding a child,

or the laying of a table –
the way the sun might slant
across the cups.

Folding a damp cloth
she catches a glimpse
of herself in the darkening

glass of an autumn evening –
listening, as the small moments
of her invisible life

are made holy;

transfigured into prayer,
by the words of a poet
she never knew.

And marvels at the way
you might put the words
for poet and great and woman

into a single sentence
that burns a hole in the dark
history of her country.

Colette McAndrew

### Gone to Earth

Three fingers curled under
show the rules of subtraction
or tap, keeping time, steering
as ash flies out the window.

Long fingers stained orange,
nails bitten to the quick
and black rimmed on hands perpetually earthed.

Fingers that worked dough for crumble
twisted a ring, restless, then
stroked my arm, the soft inside bit.

Catherine McCabe

## FATSO

There's a story of rejection
only fat girls will read.
Fat boys will read a different story
of how it feels to be nothing

and people will say
it's you
you did this
this is of your own making.
Your own special oblivion.

And the fat girls will eat in secret
away from where skinny girls eat
but these are two human hearts
with the same hunger.

Both capable of being hollowed and ragged
into jagged edges
of rage
by the same hurt.

But held to different standards.
And to all the people
who don't see who's underneath all that fat meat,
flabby and empty;
a profanity
eating itself to death.
Let me tell you a secret
*no one wants to be invisible.*

Mary McCarthy

Invoke a Whisper

Make your way
to the weeping willow,
tell it of your stolen dreams
that clung to good fortune
burnt in a crucible

under the heat of flame,
while you stood back
looking on.
How can you come back from that?
Let tears of gold fall on your cheeks.

Tell it you don't look back,
that you stroll lonely roads
daydreaming of wandering clouds,
its trailing branches full of bloom,
its wintergreen scent and a sense of belonging.

Relieved of burdens,
your secrets perfumed,
invoke a whisper to its trunk,
a rising air
you can survive.

Stand up!
You are strong.
This will be forgotten like leaves of autumn.
Let your fingers touch the bark, honour
this moment, pluck it as a harp string.

Helen McClements

MISSED CO-ORDINATES
*i.m. Donal Deery*
*died 12 January 2005, aged 29*

1

The Khao San Road is alive with fruit sellers, hawkers, noodle bars billowing white steam into the night. We forage for gifts: jade bracelets, silk wall hangings, trinket boxes of marble and finally, a small, quartz chess board for us.

Later, when we play, you are astounded when I beat you, not once but twice, toppling your king. This is new to you: you are not used to being beaten. You are not used to me, beating you.

When our boat draws up to dock on Ton Sai beach, the sky is a brooding purple bruise. The clouds unleash their torrents, and hunch backed, sarongs strung over our heads, we stumble onto sodden sand. Rain falls in slanting sheets: a Biblical curse.

We set out the board on the white of the bed, an island of stillness amid the debris of our rucksacks. I bring out my knights to swipe your bishop, but you are wise to me, picking off my pawns, my rooks, my queen.

Light dances in your eyes. 'I've found your Achilles' heel,' you say. 'You are my Achilles' heel,' I think. 'You checkmated me at hello.'

I defend and defend but defeat is inevitable. I swing my legs around; untuck the taut sheet and flick: board and pieces fly in a meteor shower of monochrome. Silence.

Then, we shriek with laughter, and put the bed to better use. Afterwards, you whisper in my ear, 'I still won, you know.'

    2

I cannot read you, plumb your depths, yet I know when you are blue and grey, contours hardening; quick to rise to my bait. I do not mean to bait you, but I do, when I order cappuccino (extra hot); linger over a muffin, (banana choc chip) in Nelson coffee shops, while you pace, backpack on, boots tightly tied, ready to hit the rock.

I am water on a balmy day, undulating, whimsical, basking in the shallows. You are land on a crisp new map, your boundaries clear, your borders defined. A strong south-easterly won't thwart your plans; your route is fixed. Take me back to Thailand: fishermen's trousers knotted at my waist, humming 'Pure Shores' by the *All Saints*, water licking my toes, hot from the sand on Railay Beach.

You can only bathe so long in the foaming surf. It's firm lines you want, not froth; enough of this dawdling by the water's edge. Plot us and see, I am the horizontal, You, the vertical axis, soaring, striding, climbing, higher and higher still, until you are off the chart.

    3

    Freefall from Tititea

Let me tell you about edges. Edges and ledges, slipping and sliding until edge disappeared and then there was only falling.

What thoughts can one manage to catch, while airborne? As my foot slipped on grass, grass which gleamed, pulled taut like skin, polished ice despite the morning sun I laughed! Until I felt the force of physics, as I gathered speed. No purchase. No comedy tree at the cliff edge to seize and catapult me back to higher ground.

My family's faces flickered as I fell; I knew I wasn't ready to leave. You reached out, grabbing me, tight around my waist as together we slid, our combined weight accelerating our descent. Two people. Two backpacks, one fall as together we clung. You said nothing.

My last glimpse of you saw urgency in your eyes. You must have seen the edge while I, sprawled as I slid, did not. One false step on a frictionless slope pared an 'us' down to an 'I'. And an upward climb to self.

Raquel McKee

## Wet Quavers

This void tastes bitter.
The chair, a sting in my throat.
Each flower unadmired, is bitterish bile.

Yet your fragrance
lingers long,
filling my lungs
with precious song.

Each wet quaver
rings with heavy love.
Memories peal, encircling like a blanket.

They come to roost
each sunset
till I swallow ...

Till purple bitter
turns orange sweet
and through the tears, I smile.

E.V. McLoughlin

## I AM NOT HERE

On my left – water.
I should know exactly
which loch or what sea.
Does it take away from something
not knowing the name?

I have seen a seal
because I was looking,
because I did not expect it,
because I paid attention.

The rain keeps going, and I have no map.
I cannot spell the name of the next station
but it sounds like woollen blankets,
currant flowers, ghosts, mud, shallow water.
I could be anywhere. But somebody laid
those tracks and I have bought a ticket.

I will add these places
to the list of names where I am not:
Whitehead, Ballycarry,
Magheramorne, Glynn ...
I am not here now, but I could
have been, I glimpsed.
I am not yours. I am
nobody's, I am just passing,
trying to pay attention.

At Larne town
the sign flashed with only one word
I understood – CLOSED.

I will take your water and air
and earth, but I will not take
your fire, your signs and your long silences –
I am just a stranger passing by.
Forgive me, I know nothing and I
do not ask. I am already here.

Liz McManus

## To Ilhan Sami Çomak

Each day, walking beside the sea,
I think of what it means to be unfree.

A winter storm can terrorise the shore
and put at risk the trawlerman and sailor.

Their choice is stark: to die or to be brave
until the sea settles again, wave on wave.

In a Turkish prison, you are braver still.
Decades have failed to break your will.

Inside you, a secret place survives:
The cosmos where your poetry thrives.

---

*Ilhan Sami Comak has been locked up in a Turkish prison for 28 years. He has said about his life: 'I work extremely hard. Inside this cordoned world surrounded by walls I work hard to hear the voice of poetry in everything.' To honour the extraordinary spirit of Ilhan Sami Comak I wrote this poem.*

Eilís Ní Anluain, a d'aistrigh

DO ILHAN SAMI ÇOMAK

Ag siúl gach lá ar an trá,
samhlaítear dom an daor.

Cuireann stoirm gheimhridh sceimhle
ar an mairnéalach agus an iascaire.

Cinneadh crua: ní mór dóibh a bheith cróga
go ligeann an fharraige fúithi, tonn ar thonn.

I ngéibheann sa Tuirc, tá tusa níos cróga fós,
blianta fada níor theip ar do mhisneach.

Maireann ionat áit rúnda:
Cosmas do chuid filíochta.

Triona Mc Murrow

## The Rag Bag

Hung on the back
of the bathroom door,
everything torn or worn
went in there.

When anyone looked for
a duster or cloth
they were sent to
root in the rag bag.

You'd use one
to wash your father's car,
clean up after the dog
and polish grubby windows.

This was before
supermarket aisles
were bursting with
Jif, Pledge and Comfort.

Did everyone cut
the gussets out of
old knickers?

Patricia Maguire

ENDA

I miss you terribly, that raw missing as when you discover something new which you crave to share and you are that almost first port of call. I discovered Hollie McNish and her poem 'When I am dead will you finally shut the fuck up' and I was blown away. I would have hit the buzzer as in the *Voice of Ireland*, made that call knowing you would identify visceral, but you are not here nor there nor anywhere tangible. No red buzzer shrills.

I have other friends, but they don't fit that wham in red-light buzzer smack, red-light humour, red-light got ya! This friendship spooled in evolve through four decades, way longer than most marriages. I, propping up a too small pram on a kerb, basket chock full, tilted with a bruiser baby and I five months 'enceinte' with another and you inquired in country lilt, wheeling your own. 'Do you need a hand?' A friendship was cast in outcast, I Belfast, you Ballinasloe on a County Wicklow turf and we found a thread that stitched lonely to kindred, and you taught a nineteen-year-old square-peg girl that raw edges can be smoothed, clematis can hide eye-sore coal black oil tanks, soup does not come from tins, light switches can dip to dim, and nothing tastes as palate cleansing as homemade mandarin cheesecake.

With you, this learning curve never stopped or dipped. We traded secrets, bolstered each other through the rocky terrain of adapt, to being a wife, a mother, spinning plates in assuming perfect, hostess with the mostest, children clipped to air-brushed *Waltons*, gardens edged to sharp, hammering ourselves into neat, sweet, upbeat puppets, mothering husbands and parents in some linear role of perfectdom and then we downed tools but never downed motherhood, even after we should have.

You ached chic and flair and classy, slim as that proverbial reed. Spilled kind and generous yet tacked to soft spoken would erupt 'fuck a duck!' And we would laugh and link arms and dreams, brush away tears and fears, people watch, raise an eyebrow to fit as, our eyes smiling knowing, but you quirked on tailored suit, I, on dungarees.

There are touches of you all around my home. 'Frame your windows, your garden is the pictorial, mirror panel that pillar to reflect the light' and when my mother died and I mourned for what had never been, you walked into my kitchen, laden with Avoca fare, this practical and generous gesture a ballast to my wooden functioning. Again, when my feet refused to carry me, you were a Constant in Caritas, and three days a week you left Shankhill for Greystones and Greystones for Rathgar and back to bring me to physio for several weeks. I was a severely indebted skittle with skittish gone!

You honed friendship to a whole new level. You brought being a wife to a whole new level with Peter in your caring, a caring that spanned. You tucked your adult children into that niche of abiding solicitude. But most of all you created a safety net for your grandchildren in a love without conditions. Danny, Lana, Rowan as in tree, Charlie-Jarlath and Rex.

Your final gift in time and strength was to Rex. A name you could only associate with a dog, a name that shone Rex Harrison to me. You planted leylandii around your home for privacy while I chopped mine down for light. You were my right-hand woman at parties. My left-hand woman in the art of clearing up, and mulled wine, and all those times in between. You were a country girl at heart in a city girl's garb. And those whom you trusted most to protect your country bolt-hole outpost, trampled your dream leaving you impoverished. In a quicksand of treachery. I don't think you ever recovered from that, though you tried. There are some treacheries that are a step too far.

There were kinks in your frame that required surgery and a few weeks before you left such a bevy of people who loved you so, you were still donning the hostess apron, the etiquette of cherry tomatoes in raspberry vinaigrette, basil and garlic and marking your calendar to make dinner for a bunch of sturdies on your birthday. Really. Wrong way round. I had booked Hunters. On your birthday you were admitted to hospital and died two weeks later. I have read your autopsy. Nothing makes sense. I think you died of tireless giving. I remember our last walk. We linked and gazed over the quietness leading to Killiney beach and we propped each other up on the changes we would make to the energy sappers.

Not for one moment did I know that you were dying, literally on your feet, but I did intuit slow down and breathlessness but took it as a baseline to kick selfless to the kerb. You handed me my Christmas present that June, when I wanted nothing. Beautiful in delicate pearl cluster earrings. Light on the lobe. There are people I know, Enda, who have failed since your passing. Peter has such strong faith and belief in your presence he finds you everywhere and in everything. We cleared out a cupboard, Peter and I, of all your out-of-date spices and I now have a picture of you to frame. Green becomes you. I miss you terribly.

I have other friends. But ...

Mari Maxwell

On Soldier's Mountain

She strides along the rocky ridge
between Benncorr and Bencollaghduff.

Pole straps slapping, whacking in late September
*wonders if she's an idiot* as winds crack in livid grey.

Heather tremors, rocks glint and sheep scuttle
bewildered at her presence.

A solo hike in the Connemara mountains.
Twelve barren peaks and valleys in a day –
the only way back is down.

She bails on first try,
as errant winds whip and slash
in rugged unstable terrain.

Four days later another pre-dawn drive
through Diamond Hill and Maam Cross.
Her head lamp bobs up the trail.

We at homebase analyse her progress,
stalk each cobalt blip on satellite tracker,
gasping the flecks onward.

*6:44am Speed 4.50MPH*
*Elevation 301.84ft*

*7:53am Speed 0.31MPH*
*Elevation 1,394.36ft*

*10:05am Speed 2.95MPH*
*Elevation 2,378.67ft*

We give our children wings
terrified at every flight.

Amanda Moloney

## Yule Eve

I forgot this wouldn't last forever,
each tradition
that I relived through you,
created for you,
that we created together,

I forgot they had a built in end,
a natural stop.

You wouldn't always believe,
couldn't.
Even if you still want to now.
I see you holding tight,
a last firm grasp,

before we both let go.

Sonya Mulligan

## The Revolution Will Be Televised

If you don't want foreigners here
and sure why would you
it's not like the Irish have left this green isle
and headed off to every corner of the world
I doubt if every single Irish family has some relative
in England or America or Australia.
Hardly.
If you don't want productive migrants here
you don't need to burn down the bloody city.
Just boycott them.

Stop sending your kids to school.
Stop going to libraries.
Stop getting taxis.
Stop ordering food for delivery.
Stop going on buses, trains or the Luas.
Stop using social media.
Stop eating in restaurants.
Stop using any or all shops.
Stop reading books or watching tv.
Stop going to college.
Stop looking for legal advice.
Stop going to the gp.
Stop going to A&E.
Stop drinking in bars.
Stop hiring painters or carpenters or builders.
Stop paying insurance.
Stop using banks.
Stop calling the fire brigade if your gaff is on fire.
Stop.

Stop being black-hooded, face-covered cowardly bowzys.
Stop pretending you care about anything other

than spouting hate and spewing poison.

Everyone knows there's nothing more annoying
than people deciding to move to our country
of a *céad míle fáilte*s
and filling jobs, providing services,
generally bringing more colour and vibrancy to the city.

This poem was brought to you
by north face and Canada goose
no ordinary decent human beings
were harmed during the making of this poem.

Mitzie Murphy

## Don't Tell

*I'm not allowed to tell*, I screamed at the wall. I had woken up with the same knot I had fallen asleep with. It was twisting into a tangle. I could feel it pushing and stretching the skin under my torn red t-shirt. I clasped my sweaty hands together and banged them on my head. I rocked while whispering to myself *I am not allowed to tell* in many different voices. I talked out loud to the wall. *My family have secrets*. If you were to lay them down back-to-back, they would stretch all the way across the Nullarbor Plain. The wall listened, but the coil in my belly grew. I sat up. I knew I had to move. I had to find my way out of this stinking bed. I swung around and shocked myself with the sound my feet made when they hit the cold tiles. I had not felt my feet on the floor in a long time. My torso trembled, and the knot swelled. It travelled until it arrived in my mouth. My tongue forced the dirty black secrets to fall to the ground. Somehow, later, I found the door.

Anne Murray

## Nearly Me
*after sculpture*, 'Woman in a Bomb Blast', F.E. McWilliams, 1974

Wandering the city centre that day,
three teenage girls.
Coffee,
a cool thing to do,
and we nearly did, but hesitated
and debated if there was time –
it was busy and already
late afternoon in Castle Lane,
our train at the GNR a good
ten minutes brisk walk away,
time running out.

Our mothers would be worried,
we promised
we'd be home.
We'd do the Abercorn
another day.

We race to Wallis
for a quick jaunt 'round the maxi coats
in our midis and minis
trying the purple fantasy on
in the changing rooms,
to see who we could be
with endless pocket money.

That quiet happy hush
of being young
and having fun,
before the blast.
BOOM.

Seconds later,
the sound of smashed
droplets of glass, lifting into the air,
crashing, crash.
Shhhh.

People pause.
Stilted. Stiff necks,
ears ringing, eyes open.
Then the crying.
People running from,
people running to.

Bríd Ní Chomáin

## WAITING ON A TEXT

Waiting on a text back
is like listening to an older lady
talk about the current state of affairs
how nobody takes pride
in their work anymore
tell you about her favourite stockpot
'not like the muck they make these days
a well-made pot for life'
that she's had since the night
she first laid back and thought of Ireland
and her husband with shaky hands
fondled and fumbled
and she wondered
if this was really what it's all about

waiting on a text back
is like the rush to get on the ten past six bus
on a Tuesday
teenagers edging their shoulders
around you
the entire population of the bus stop
joined at various body parts
moving as one to the 2ft gap
as if the bus will take off flying
at any second
as if the seats will disappear
if one is not the first on
and you're there
doing the same stupid shit
as the rest of the idiots
and judging them harshly
as you do

waiting on a text back
is stubbing your toe repeatedly
on alternating feet
so that just as the rush of pain in one
starts to dull
it's renewed afresh in the other
it's a needle plunging
into fingernails
it's your shin bashed on the leg
of the bed
it's standing up suddenly
in the kitchen
only for your forehead to collide
with the corner of the press
you left open

it's every lurch in the pit of your stomach
every person who hurt you
every time you felt small
it's the year and a half you starved
so you could look in the mirror
while wearing jeans
it's the evening
after being home all day
you're so numb you can't
watch tv even
so you talk to someone
who isn't there
and wank
until you cry

it's returning to square one
over and over and over
again and again
and working hard
to remind yourself

that last time
each time
you climbed back up
a couple of notches
eventually

Ciara Ní É

U̲n̲t̲i̲t̲l̲e̲d̲

when their mother found her voice

she began to ask
why
her five children
whose DNA she had knitted
with the pith of her bones
who she'd pushed into the world
with a battle cry
why
they did not bear her name
why
her name would die with her
why

one of her children makes a change
and is blasted every other day
with "How does your poor dad feel
that you're not taking his name?"
by people who dance on the point
without seeing it

only ever asking
"how does he feel?"
and never
"how does she?"

Helena Nolan

ICELAND
*for Lucy Caldwell*
"This is an island and therefore unreal" – Auden

They say the women who went there
lost their shadows on the journey,
spent the rest of their lives searching,
always just missing the glimpse
of who they were before.

Now, when women go there
we feel at home, slip easily
into the old forsaken shadows,
claim them for our own, mistaking
light for darkness and the dark for light.

Once, one woman, in those old days
turned so fast she thought she saw
her future, but it was only her past,
vanishing so quickly it left a trail
as soft as breathsmoke on a frozen day.

Maria Noonan-McDermott

## The Red Chair

A wash of colour, a few perpendicular lines
and the room is staged.
With charcoal, I block in the chair
with large sweeping marks.
The structure, sturdy and solid,
the only thing grounded when all else is fleeting.

The red chair,
which wasn't red at all,
but as time went on, every shade
and variation became red
and she was drawn to it like a moth to light.

I sketch her face, a noble face,
skin like parchment. Her eyes glazed
over and staring, lips thin with an almost smile,
hair long, loose the way she liked it.

I draw her comfortably into her red chair
and stand back. Hmm, is there something not quite right?
I wipe it clean and start again.

I close my eyes and imagine my hands
gliding down the length of her fragile frame.
It is as familiar to me as my own.
I know every joint and muscle
from daily care and love.

Again, I turn to the canvas and paint with vigour,
recalling each limb from head to toe
until I have captured her essence.
Her soft delicate bones, skin so translucent
she should surely disappear!

But, there is no fear as she sits
within the passage of time
in the company of the spirits.
She lives each moment with reverence.
No past, no future.
Each heartbeat, a precious sacred gift.

Grace O'Doherty

DECLINATION OF BEAUTY

The street wins most polluted
each year, last corridor
of dirty cars prohibited
from entering the city proper.

Particles from factories accompany
the east wind, get trapped
and printed by rain on windows
it makes no sense to clean.

The neighbours' full-moon lampshade
is lit at night, and days
when rain rinses dog shit
and discarded meals to the gutter.

In the boxes *zum Verschenken*
most things are broken:
damp book, husk of shelving,
spoiled mirror, divorced sock.

An imposter blue sky arrives with sirens.
We keep the windows closed.
The neighbours pull their drapes across,
or they leave and turn the moon off.

Lauren O'Donovan

To Mrs Brown, my Fifth-Year Biology Teacher

I still remember
how you would burst into a drowsy classroom
with mud on your boots and hands full of ferns
so fresh they dripped spiders and dew.

You told us to trace our fingertips
along the sporangium underneath a leaf
and explained how each tiny spore would sail
on rain and find its own way to new soil

where it would grow strong, despite the struggle.
And I did struggle, but not in your class.
Even the girls who smacked chewing gum,
wore makeup and rolled their skirts into belts

listened when you demonstrated how to hold
the scalpel and carefully slice through layers
of sclera, choroid, nerves and ligaments
into the thick jelly of a cow's eye,

explaining that vision occurs in the brain
whereas the eye is an organ of innocent parts
incapable of casting judgement.
You were my teacher for a single year

before mom moved me to a new school.
I swapped my uniform for jeans, traded
the sneers of girls I'd known since Montessori
for the empty smiles of almost-women

and an ache for oblivious teenage boys.
Just one year, but still, whenever I study,

I see mud splatters and dewdrops on the page
as I draw and redraw diagrams:

the structure of the eye,
the life cycle of the fern.

Bláithín O'Reilly Murphy

## My First Born

The bang, pop, bang hit my ears
as I realise I'm leaking.
A fear grips me, stuns me.
No one prepares you for this.

There is a cold realisation
or perhaps that's the sterile hospital chair.
Surely they will know what to do.
I sit, nod and stare; my (new) world collapses.

I know you are on your way,
they don't believe me.
My body knows what to do;
there is no pain, no pushing, no crying.

There are ten tiny fingers and toes.
And a heartbeat, all wrapped in 101g of perfection.
But; all we take home is a birth and death certificate.
No one prepares you for this.

Sarah Padden

How to Commit Genocide

First, silence the poets and journalists, use attack drones and be sure to bomb their family home as well, this method can also be used for hospital consultants. Use Twitter/X to undermine their posthumous reputation and cause doubt in compliant countries. Next, create a famine to destroy social solidarity and turn adult against child for a bowl of Quaker soup. As the first images of emaciation appear, get a uniformed government spokesman to deny food and water shortages exist, and blame the UN, Red Crescent and natives for eating too much. Withhold fuel and oil for water pumps, thirst is a quicker solution and less apparent on TikTok.

Shoot solar panels on church rooftops with tank shells, use army snipers to prevent elders leaving pews. Get an elected official to declare no Christians remain, pre-emptively, in the manner of a modern prophet to ensure the full eradication of this most ancient of Christian communities occurs unnoticed. It must be concluded before celebrations of the Bethlehem nativity, to stop the Prince of Peace reminding our war-benefactors of the birth of helpless infants in precarious Palestinian caves.

Keep the population on the move with orders to flee to a safer, confined place and cause mass homelessness, then drop two-thousand-pound bombs on tents in UN hospital car parks and school gardens. Absolutely refute official figures of bodies recovered from rubble and counted for accuracy, especially mothers. Use bulldozers to uproot graves of the newly-buried and, if denials won't work as it was already posted, get a suave spokesman to say in eloquent English it's because a utility tunnel beneath the graves could be used to hide people. Be specific with the word *hostage*, as it could be applied to anyone unable to escape bombs, slaughter and famine in a closed enclave on the Egyptian border.

When the ambassador cries at the UN Council because a girl called *Dunia*, whose name means *the realm of the whole world* was orphaned and pulled from rubble when her home was bombed, still had hope of a life even after her leg was amputated, but was killed a few weeks later in her hospital bed – cut the internet and power lines. Stop local journalists interviewing children for CNN and silence the poet. Do not let any ambassador hear the name *Dunia* before the UN Council votes to demand a ceasefire by all sides and the protection of civilians in wartime.

Celina Papendorf

YOU

You are in this cave again
with the darkness known by a hundred names:
depression, exhaustion, burnout – yet all of them
fail to describe the way you've changed.
And here I am, watching you,
helpless and useless.

You – who was always up for an adventure,
now you never leave the flat.
You – whose flat mirrors your state of mind,
lately you rearrange non-stop and it is now
made out of a hundred small construction sites.
You – who laughs out loud a lot,
but the way your face moves seems different,
a bit more worried, a bit greyer.
You – whom I am watching,
even though I want to hold and protect you.
You – who I hope will be fine,
but lately my definition of fine seems to be tested.
You – who I am watching with faith,
yet unsure if you do the same.
You – at war with your own self and the world.

A war I am ready for, dressed as a soldier.
I want to join in the fight, but can't,
because I neither see the haunting dreams
nor seem to find my way to the battlefield you are on.

"It will be fine," I said,
but now I know it won't
because 'fine' is just a word
whose meaning we forgot over time.

It's happening in your head.
But how can it be only in the head
when you've changed so visibly?
Where did the bubbly version I know so well go?

Here I am, reaching out, with my arm in the air,
trying to stroke you with my fingertips,
trying to whisper that I am not leaving,
that I trust
you will endure this war
and survive this year.

Here I am, unsure about my own words,
just trying to get you back,
but my arm stops mid-air,
untouching and unsure.
If I wake you
am I ripping you from peace
or am I helping you
to escape yet another nightmare?

Saakshi Patel

BANU

Thrust into motherhood, young and unaware
of her own date of birth, she daydreams
of distant travels to a place without care:
perhaps the one pictured on her pack of cream-
filled biscuits, a treat for herself and her two kids,
kicking a deflated football to keep entertained
till her return. Home was rusted rods, slid
upright under blue plastic tarp, maintained
before the threatened shelter was uprooted,
moving the family to the construction site
her husband works at, breathing air polluted
by dust and debris, as watchman for the night.
In sporadic sleep, she's a girl again, committed
to her wonderland with cream biscuits, unlimited.

Ruth Quinlan

## A Poet's Inscription
Heinrich Boll's Cottage, Achill Island
*i.m. Tom Duddy (1950–2012)*

I find it in the pages of a book
that I pluck like an errant feather
from the plumage of a library –
a copy of his first collection,
dedicated to this writer's home.

I remember an angular man
in the vaulted box of a lecture hall,
begging us not to bury words as he did
but dig them up, dust them off,
balance them carefully as dry-stone walls.

Later, we sipped our beers,
talking with and about the man
who'd thrown a match into the pools
of petrol we'd been sitting on, complacent
about the time we'd left to light them.

I feel the singe of that incendiary
call as I sit at the desk
he wrote at, look out the window
through which he watched storms
scrape themselves on the blackthorn fence.

I like to think of him here in Achill,
the year before he passed, roaming
old bog roads with a notebook,
the high June sun blinding him,
hiding the destination that lay ahead.

Mary Ringland

WOOED

I watch our laburnum tree's hollow trunk,
a testament to three score years, and think
you and the tree have spanned the same.

It's flounce of silk dipped in turmeric, blinked
the sunlight in and wooed two newlyweds to bid on it.
Today in our living room, your birthday cards attend

the tambour clock. Its ticking has lulled us into thinking
that if we wound it, it would do our bidding,
but not so loud as to quell your gentle whistling

and the rhythmic tapping of your shoe.
The spin wails, the cycle's over,
I drag out limp sleeves for the week to come.

Rebecca Ruane

## A 28-Year-Old-Woman Buys a Field in Galway

they've accepted my bid
I cry, take a picture of myself
against wallpaper green fields and sheep

my Father gets the map
through two pairs of layered Tesco glasses reads;
*the first known person to own that field*
*is from 1726       ah yeah, an Irishman*
*wouldn't have hung that gate*
*that's a landlord's gate*

my sister says congratulations
by referring to me as
*the landed gentry*

I tell my neighbour
and the height of his eyebrows
says it all

I tell my counsellor
she says *wow*
I say *scam*

I haven't yet allowed myself
the emotion of audacity
I have never felt like I could possess anything
especially the joy of my own life

I walk through the ruin
of the Big House in the back field
my parents repeat an old joke,
so Hiberno it's barely in English

I ask them *explain it*

their faces twist away from me
until I press the truth out of them
they suppose it's about how
*the landlord took brides*
*on the wedding night*

my family have been here
longer than recorded maps

the stones
come up out of the ground
and answer my questions

my Mother asks
*what would your Grandfather say*
*if he saw you in this field, if he was alive?*

he only finished paying the land commission in 1965

I sit with an ancient sob
from someone inside me

who owns it?
my Great Grandmother
starting with 10 chickens
lived to see her son
piss the price of 40 acres
*up a-gin a wall*

who owns it?
last year I sowed a field of Kerr's Pinks
I watched the field powder its own nose
I let them lye back into the soil
said *goodnight*
*you don't need to work so hard*

who owns the sob?
I tell my friend
*I feel like the Bull McCabe*
and that *all this*
*has nothing to do*
*with anyone who is alive*

apart from me
and my family
and my field

D'or Seifer

## My 100th Attempt at a Love Poem

In the future I will wake to the whisper of waves,
the wind's howling through rocks,
the rumble of tide's tympani against cave walls,
the spectrum of a cymbal's featherlight decay.

I will hold my cobalt mug in softness,
receive it ensconced by the window,
wear garments that enrobe,
soft as the fearful promises of a beginning.

In the future I will swing out
still cackling maniacally as you push,
hands like the warm curves of sand
on the beaches of my childhood.

You will come around to sit in stillness,
the BBC's *In Our Time*,
a shell playing, lulling the evening,
and your bicuspid baby tooth
emerging in that special quiet
that promises a future.

Mary Shannon

## On the Fourteen-Forty-Five Iarnród Éireann to Malahide

We talk of the musicality of language
as the train chugs and clatters along iron rails
bedded on stone track ballast.
Its wailing whistle drifts over
Killester, Harmonstown and Raheny.

Rhythmic our voices revel in long-spun stories
with throats well-oiled from quaffing cocktails
in the Saints and Scholars Bar of Wynn's Hotel.

After Kilbarrack, our voices dwindle
in sound and timbre passing by
Donaghmede and Clongriffin.
By Portmarnock they swell again,
in a chorus of Nordie exuberance,
as the fourteen-forty-five Iarnród Éireann
draws closer to the Grand Hotel in Malahide.

Katie Sheehan

BENEDICTION

I asked the earth to find me
a home, and she set me down

amid the gorse. I asked
the earth to keep me. She left me

gold, too rooted in the land
to trade. I asked the earth

to give me cover. Each leaf
she grew – a whetted spine.

Each stem – a wind-hewn rafter.

Cassie Smith-Christmas

## TAHLEQUAH J35

Tá a leanbh marbh fós
ar a srón
tonn tar éis toinne
míle tar éis míle

agus na deora ag rith:
salann go salann
uisce go huisce
go deo.

Agus a leanbh fós ar a srón.

Seo ár saol,
saol na míolta móra:

gan bhradáin
gan bhia
gan bheatha.

Agus a leanbh fós ar a srón.

Amy Smyth

STILL

When the world is still.
Still quiet, still asleep.
Soft chirping, gentle snoring,
quiet coffee and delicate sunlight.

My world is seldom still these days –
still predictable, still controllable,
but rarely quiet and never delicate.

My mind drifts to when my world was too still,
a whimsical backward glance at a life, even then,
I knew was not for me.
Now sitting in a life I am unsure is for me
still.

Eilis Stanley

A Dangerous Thing

She said she picked wrong ones,
a dangerous thing, a wedding dress
descent with Don
was a slow walk on a frozen lake
from chest thumps,
facial slaps to bone breaks
and fractured skull.

Every day escalations
drove her inside,
closed doors,
turned off the lights,
made her homeless in her house.

A knuckle to cheek
could arrest breath,
bring compliance.
She took care of time taken
with friends on the phone,
minded her smile at the mailman,
never talked to strangers.
Her limbs bruise maps of his hands.
Scarves, cardigans hid
the geography of daily life.
Sunglasses.

Once she made a run for it.
Took Amtrak, Texas to Maine,
watched two thousand miles
of America flash under train wheels
as she sat, her two sons beside her.
They ate hot dogs and fries,

slept like orphan puppies,
heads laid against shoulders
or shaky train windows.

She sought help from her big brother,
Jimmy, who lived in Bideford.
He'd battled booze, married late,
has some savvy, she thought.
But Jimmy ordered her home
so Don could put a jess on her.
See, she said, *always the wrong ones.*

Sarah Strong

## Billy's Room

I don't remember how my mother punished me for stealing the curtains off her lover's bedroom window and making them into bell bottoms but I do see myself on a ladder unpicking the brass hooks from the pelmet with care. I hurl the cloth into a great heap. The burgundy material which I crave so much lies in fronds on the floor. I wield a pair of scissors, the shears gleaming. I place my paper pattern on the carpet, align pins, sew tailor tacks. I feel powerful and spiteful. I make the first cut, and metal and material meet like sparrows tussling in a hedge. I plough furrow after furrow, up one leg to my vulva and down the other side to my foot. In the stale room, the pattern pieces are quiet. Will they leap up and kill me, enact my mother's certain rage? I remove her Singer sewing machine from her locked cupboard. I gather my wilful work. I cut and sew and construct my costume. I stand before her tarnished mirror. I settle my shocking-pink hat with the wide brim sent from Carnaby Street on my head and saunter with panache to the Bamboo Café in Dún Laoghaire.

Lila Stuart

## Your Way

I feel you at my elbow,
your warm breath near my ear,
as I weigh and measure
the makings of soda bread.
For you it was fistfuls of this,
dollops of that, pinches of the other,
rubbed between finger and thumb.
I haven't got your confidence –
always checking in cookery books –
longing for your nod to tell me.

Whisper in my ear your recipe for
recreating the essence of those we miss.

Csilla Toldy

## MIDSUMMER REUNION IN FOUR CHAPTERS

1

*The Secret*

The rabbits floated on a makeshift boat,
white-purple sky glinting on the river.
Surely, I was one of them. What coat,
brown, black or white? It didn't matter.
It is enough to say we were many,
a team of dreamers and wanna-bees.
We played: perfect father, mother, baby –
our mundane worries had butterfly wings.
I cooked you a star soup and you drank it.
It might have been the only nourishment
on the whole tenement – our sweet secret.
"Make us real!" I whispered to the wind
and the magic of love blew my mind
– for a moment I'll never forget.

2

*Forgotten*

For a moment I'll never forget,
the sea with its azure sheen caressed
my senses. In the old Jewish district,
standing on a balcony over Nice
the sun tamed the wind or vice
versa, the wind crept under my sundress?
I felt tender, blessed, solemnly grateful
for living in a world of tolerance
where it is my birthright to be peaceful
and I am not treated with ignorance.

But soon I walked with disturbed contentment:
makeshift, cardboard beds wedged on the pavement,
the homeless sleeping to forget their day
while I, like a cat tip-toed on my way.

3

*Remembered*

While I, like a cat tip-toed on my way,
lavender odour crept into my nose
transporting my mind to an old school day
when we escaped to movies from the throes
of stressing teachers, screaming "Help!" for joy.
Our egos were slumbering deep, buried
under insecurities to decoy
when we'd reach maturity. Soon, carried
away to the colosseum of work
where competition made us clueless,
numb to the hurts we suffered or caused
attacking our hearts – to what success?
Then, in the forced pause, we remembered
the reckless love that binds us together.

4

*Redeemed*

The reckless love that binds us together
is a ghost in the corridors of our
memory that summons the truth-lover
in all of us. Yet, the freedom of our
world is limiting. We know nothing but
signs that direct or misinterpret – more
or less, and if we're not given the gut
to trust we get lost in the metaphor,
the maze of signs; our little, instinctive id-s

waiting for the super-ego to show
which way to go; when nobody provides.
Fool's gold is the cargo, but the slaves row
to the lull of redeeming anecdotes:
The rabbits floated on a makeshift boat ...

Enya Trofimoff

## Rosemary Breath

I lie next to you,
our bodies relaxed under woolly covers.
You sleep, features drawn from stars.

My hand stretches over your chest,
tasting your warmth,
the move of your breath under my palm.

A gentle breeze parts the curtains
bringing the familiar scent
of your shampoo.

I angle my body closer to you
always in that single direction.
Sweet seconds stop for us.

You stir, lips delicately part,
eyes focusing on me
before a shy blush dusts your cheeks.

You pull me close, hands in my hair, face
pressed to your neck. You whisper a confession
I have heard a thousand times before.

One that I will answer, without doubt.

Carmel Uí Cheallaigh

## Dreoilín Dreoilín Rí na nÉan

A luaithe a chonaic mé thú,
smaoinigh mé siar ar Lá Fhéile Stiofáin
ag siúl inár gcóiriú ó bhaile go baile
ag bailiú na bpinginí chun tú a chur

níor lig Mam dúinn fíoréan a cheapadh
sháigh sí dhá chleite isteach i bhfata
is chuir an 'corp' isteach i bpróca
is scairt inár ndiaidh, "Go dté sibh slán!"

Le damhsa is ceol is gáire san aer
isteach linn sna bailte, sna tithe tábhairne
le ruaille buaille is rannta d'amhráin
cuireadh thart buicéad don bhailiúchán

anois tá go leor de na cleamairí imithe
ach maireann an chuimhne, tá an traidisiún beo
nach muide a bhí chomh haerach leis na héin
na blianta ó shin i gContae Mhaigh Eo!

Emi Uyematsu

## Sitting Down in the Shower

I sit beneath the spray
the too long shower curtain suctions to my skin
threatening to suffocate me if I do not drown

when I press my thighs together
water pools between them
rising over my dark pubic hair
rivers trail across my hipbones
*it's like geography or some shit*
like the lake that fills between my cupped palms
as I gulp down mouthful after mouthful
of *ew that's warm*

and the flavour of everyone telling me
*don't drink that*
is sweeter and more refreshing
than the crisp cold stream
that pisses out of the fridge downstairs

Morgan L. Ventura

SPOLIA

1

Photos litter bookshelves that sink like ships into Victorian
wooden floors. Ghosts rattle radiators on the anniversary
of a death, of a birth, of a marriage, of a divorce.
Chicago, forever my memory palace,
riddled with certificates, petitions.
Papers, legal proceedings
are artefacts – authentic, disputed,
spolia of kinship gone awry.

2

My body is stained glass,
my body is a hieroglyph.
I think of the fire my great-grandfather fought
after leaving Ireland, I think of the fire that might consume
my body when I die one day. And when I do die
will it be there, will I be home, and what is home?
Chicago cannot be home because I reject it.
And its heritage is a splintered gavel,
cereal milk, salted wounds, and the husk of a man
whom I love and who could never be brave and who
I call my father.

3

Hyde Park's architecture groans
under bullets and intellectuals.
I can never sleep here, burdened by a pedigree
when I no longer wanted it
and when those I loved were no longer

around. Birthday cards planted like adoring tombstones,
old keys that open nothing to nowhere.
*I love you* I whisper into the darkness. In the garden
wisteria answers but the words are lost, swallowed
by the absence that follows me and sits on my chest.

## About the Contributors

MAEVE ABYSS is a poet and performer originally from the USA. She has performed in Appalachia, Romania, and Ireland where she currently lives. She has started a poetry collective called Story Riot that will be touring around festivals in Ireland in 2024. She is currently working on her first novel and believes that pigeons and rats will one day inherit the earth.

SÍLE AGNEW was born in Dublin, lives in Kildare and loves any time she is lucky enough to spend in Wexford where she wanders, watches and writes poetry, prose and short stories about characters who explore everyday events that conceal the internal conflicts of the heart and soul. She is a watercolourist and a producer.

MICHELLE IVY ALWEDO is a poet of Ugandan descent who has been published in anthologies across Africa and North America. She enjoys theatre, people's pets, and intimate conversations with strangers. Alwedo facilitates workshops on narrative reconstruction for survivors of trauma. She runs a poetry and print greetings card store.

Limerick-born MARIE BASHFORD-SYNNOTT (MA Women's Studies) is married with four children and lives in Skerries. Currently working on a biography of the Irish writer Annie Smithson for Arlen House, she has won a Society of Irish Playwrights award for a one-act play and is preparing her full-length play, *Ladies Do*, for production. She has published poetry in *The Salmon* and *A New Ulster* and was a prize-winner in the George Moore Short Story Competition. Her trilogy of historical novels was serialized in *Ireland's Own*.

TRISH BENNETT hails from the Leitrim/Fermanagh border. She worked as an engineer for years before she began to write and perform. In 2022, Bennett won the New Roscommon Writing Award. She also received a General Arts Award, funded by the Arts Council of Northern Ireland & the National Lottery, and a Cill Rialaig Residency from the Irish Writers Centre. Her micro-pamphlet, *Borderlines*, is published by Hedgehog Press (2019).

CLAIRE BLENNERHASSETT is a writer, performer and multidisciplinary artist from Kildare. Her work is inspired by themes of nature, joy, belonging and colour, with a side of quirkiness, the ethereal and the surreal. She believes in magic, wonder, creativity and fun, and in the healing powers of love and a cat.

From Donegal, SARA BOYCE writes poetry and short stories. She was shortlisted for Aurivo North West Words Poetry Competition 2019, longlisted for the Seamus Heaney Award for New Writing 2018 and had a poem published in *Her Other Language* (Arlen House, 2020). She's been awarded three bursaries from the Irish Writers Centre.

YVONNE BOYLE's poetry and short stories are published in a variety of magazines, books and anthologies including the *Bangor Literary Journal, Dunfanaghy Writers Anthologies* and *Washing Windows Too*. She won the inaugural Sam Overend Award for New Poetry in 2016 after winning the Poetry House Poetry Slam. She was an ACNI Support for the Individual Artist (SIAP) awardee 2018/9. She is a Causeway Coast and Glens Councillor.

CAROLINE BRACKEN's poems have been published or forthcoming in *Poetry Wales, New England Review, Belfield Literary Review*, the *Irish Times, The North, Gutter*, the *Honest Ulsterman, Poetry Jukebox, Best New British & Irish Poets 2019–2021, Washing Windows Too, Skylight 47* and *Howl*. She was granted an Agility Award by the Arts Council in 2021 and an Emerging Artist Award by DLR Arts Office in 2022. She was selected for the Poetry Ireland Introductions Series 2018.

MARIE BREEN-SMYTH lives in Meenaclady, County Donegal and in County Derry where she was born and has returned after living in Wales, England and the United States. Although her work and publications have largely been social and political research, journalism and some film work, since the 1970s she has published poetry erratically in *The Salmon, Poetry Ireland Review, Fingerpost, Fortnight* and in North American journals. She studied creative writing at Harvard, the Seamus Heaney Centre for Poetry and Grub Street, Boston and was a 1999 recipient of a Cill Rialaig Residency.

CLODAGH BRENNAN HARVEY is a specialist in Irish oral narrative, though poetry is now the focus of her writing. She has published in a number of anthologies and journals, including *Washing Windows, Too* and *III*. Her poem 'Queue' was shortlisted for the 2015 Bridport Prize, and 'If not *El Niño*, what?' was shortlisted for the Seamus Heaney Award for New Writing (2017).

JACQUIE BURGESS is a medical herbalist and therapist living in County Carlow. She is the author of two published books on crystal healing. Her first poem was published in *Washing Windows Too* in 2022. Jacquie is a great lover of nature – she tends her garden, keeps bees, celebrates the festivals of the Celtic Wheel of the Year and enjoys painting and illustration.

LYNN CALDWELL's work has been published in *Poetry Ireland Review*, *Writing Home* and *The Book of Life* (Dedalus), *Cyphers*, *Crannóg*, *Crosswinds Poetry Journal*, *The Irish Times* and *Aesthetica*'s creative writing anthology; and has featured on *Sunday Miscellany*. Now a Dubliner, Lynn is a Canadian calling Ireland her second home.

MARY ROSE CALLAGHAN was born in Dublin. She has written nine novels, including *Billy, Come Home* and *A Bit of a Scandal*. *Awkward Women*, a collection of interconnected short stories, was recently published by Arlen House. Her memoir, *The Deep End*, is available from Menma Publications. She lives in Bray, County Wicklow.

MARION CLARKE is a short form poet from Warrenpoint, County Down. Featuring regularly in journals and anthologies, her poetry is included in the first two collections of haiku from Ireland. *Financial Times* 'Haiku Poet in the City' winner 2015, Marion combines her visual art and photography with haiku to produce haiga and photo haiku, and she was awarded 'Master of the Month' in NHK World-Japan's programme *Haiku Masters*, 2018. In 2020 she was runner up in the UHTS's *Samurai* Haibun

Contest and Grand Prize Winner in the Setouchi-Matsuyama Photo Haiku Competition 2022.

SUSAN CONDON holds an MA in Creative Writing from Dublin City University. Short stories and poems have won awards, including first prize in the Jonathan Swift Award. Writing has been published in *Boyne Berries, Flash Fiction* magazine (USA), *Flash Flood* journal, *Live Encounters* (Indonesia) and *My Weekly* (UK).

MAUREEN DALY: I came late to poetry. I have been featured in *Revival, Cyphers*, Rush poetry publication (Jane Clarke, editor). Also featured in many anthologies, including *Romantic Options* (Dedalus).

SORCHA DE BRÚN has published poems and short stories in various anthologies, and her work features on the primary curriculum. A recipient of the Foras na Gaeilge Award, the Máirtín Ó Cadhain Short Story Award and Oireachtas na Gaeilge awards, she has translated the work of numerous German poets for the *Dánnerstag* Irish-German poetry project. Sorcha is completing her monograph on masculinities in Irish language writing, forthcoming from Arlen House.

HELEN DEMPSEY from Rush, has won Fingal Libraries' Poetry Day competition, 2018, 2021; and Jonathan Swift Poetry Competition, 2023. Her poems have appeared in *Live Encounters, A New Ulster* and the Ireland Chair of Poetry commemorative anthology. *Planting a Pear Tree* is her debut collection due from Revival Press in 2024.

DOREEN DUFFY (MA Creative Writing DCU), studied at NUIM, UCD and Oxford Online. Published in *Washing Windows Too, Poetry Ireland Review, Beyond Words Literary Magazine, The Galway Review, Flash Fiction USA, Live Encounters,* the *Incubator Journal, Ireland's Own Anthology, Woman's Way,* the *Irish Times, The Storms,* among others. Pushcart nominated, she won The Jonathan Swift Award and was presented with The Deirdre Purcell Cup at the Maria Edgeworth Literary Festival. Shortlisted in The RTÉ Short Story Competition, her story 'Tattoo' was broadcast on RTÉ Radio One.

GER DUFFY lives in County Waterford. Her poems have been published by Viking Press, Voxgalvia, The Waxed Lemon, Drawn to the Light Press, *Southword, The Ekphrastic Review, The Bangor Literary Journal, The Stony Thursday Book*, The Milk House, *Local Wonders* (Dedalus Press), *Cathal Bui* anthology, *In the Midst* anthology and *Voices from the Land* anthology. She has won prizes at Westival Poetry Competition, the Goldsmiths' International Poetry Competition, the Red Line Poetry Competition, Fingal Libraries Poetry Competition and the Frances Ledwidge Poetry Awards. She has received mentorships in poetry from the Munster Literature Centre and the National Mentoring Scheme.

Born in 1954, CATHERINE DUNNE is the author of one work of non-fiction and twelve novels. Shortlisted for Novel of the Year and the International Strega Prize, she won the Giovanni Boccaccio International Prize for Fiction in 2013. Her latest, *A Good Enough Mother*, won the European Rapallo Prize 2023.

MICHELINE EGAN was born in Castlebar, County Mayo. She started her career on provincial newspapers and has worked with words since 1982. She has an MA and an MFA in writing from UCD. She is currently doing a PhD with the University of Limerick. She was awarded first prize in the Phoenix Literary Festival and was a joint recipient of the Caroline Walsh bursary. Her core themes centre around mothers, mental health, legacies and country & western music grounded in Irish towns.

ATTRACTA FAHY, psychotherapist (MAW NUIG 2017). Winner, Trócaire Poetry Ireland Competition 2021. *Irish Times*, New Irish Writing 2019, Pushcart & Best of Web nominee, shortlisted for Fish International Poetry Competition 2022, OTE 2018 New Writer, Allingham Poetry both 2019 & 2020, Write by the Sea Writing Competition 2021, Dedalus Press Mentoring Programme 2021. Her poems have been published in many magazines and anthologies at home and abroad. Fly on the Wall Poetry published her debut chapbook collection *Dinner in the Fields*, in

March 2020. She received an Agility Award from the Arts Council 2022, and is presently working towards a full collection.

HELEN FALLON was born in Monaghan and now lives in Maynooth. She was selected for Poetry Ireland's Introductions series 2022. She has published poems in *A New Ulster*, *Skylight47*, *Chasing Shadows*, *Future Perfect: Fifty Award-Winning Poems* and *Sparks of the Everyday: Poetry Ireland Introductions 2022*. She retired in 2022 from her post as Deputy University Librarian at Maynooth University. Prior to that she worked at Dublin City University and the University of Sierra Leone.

CAROLE FARNAN started writing poetry on her return to her native Belfast in 2012. Since then her work has featured in the *Honest Ulsterman*, *A New Ulster*, *Bangor Literary Journal*, *Corncrake* magazine and on the Poetry Jukebox, as well as in several anthologies. She has won the An Culturlann Poetry Prize (English category) and The Féile an Pobhail short story competition.

TANYA FARRELLY is the author of four books. Her debut short fiction collection *When Black Dogs Sing* (Arlen House, 2016) was longlisted for the Edge Hill Short Story Prize and named winner of the Kate O'Brien Award 2017. Two novels: *The Girl Behind the Lens* (2016) and *When Your Eyes Close* (2018) were published by Harper Collins. She curated and edited *The Music of What Happens*, an anthology of poems, stories and essays published in aid of Purple House Cancer Support Centre (New Island, 2020). Her latest book is the short fiction collection *Nobody Needs to Know* (Arlen House, 2021).

DEIRDRE FLAHERTY BRADY is a lecturer at Mary Immaculate College, and has published in international journals on the subject of Irish culture and women writers of the mid-twentieth-century. She also writes plays. She is the author of *Literary Coteries and the Irish Women Writers' Club (1933–1958)* (Liverpool University Press, 2021).

BERNADETTE FOX: I am thrilled to say that *The Everyday Fantastic* is my first poem to be published. Ireland's Own published my memoir story entitled *Cherry Blossoms* in their 2022 anthology of winning short stories. I enjoy being part of a Creative Writers' group in Dún Laoghaire Rathdown Public libraries. I am a retired librarian.

AMY GAFFNEY hails from Kildare and is a graduate of UCD's Creative Writing MA. Her poetry is published in *Poetry Ireland Review*, the *Irish Times* New Irish Writing and in *Washing Windows Too*. Amy's short story *Mother May I* was shortlisted for the Irish Book Awards Short Story of the Year in 2019. Her debut novel *The Moonlight Gardening Club* is published by Avon Books in 2023 under the pseudonym Rosie Hannigan.

SHAUNA GILLIGAN writes fiction, non-fiction and poetry. Her latest book is *Mantles* (Arlen House, 2021), a collaboration with visual artist Margo McNulty, exploring heritage and place symbolising the sacred feminine and Brigid. She has received numerous awards including a Cecil Day Lewis Award (2015), Creative Ireland Award (2022) and a Brigid 1500 Arts and Creativity Grant (2023). She is interested in narrative and history, the perception and interpretation of body, and the crossover of artistic processes.

AIMEE GODFREY is a disabled poet, whose work largely focuses on how disability intersects with and impacts other facets of the human condition. Her work has previously been published by *Dodging the Rain*, *The Stinging Fly*, *Púca*, *Banshee*, *ROPES*, *Tir na nOg* and the *Honest Ulsterman*.

ANITA GRACEY has been published in *Poetry Ireland Review*, *Washing Windows*, *Washing Windows Too*, *Abridged*, *Honest Ulsterman*, *Poetry NI*, *Poets' Republic*, *Fly on the Wall*, *Blue Nib*, *Culture Matters*, *CAP*, *Bangor Literary Review*, *Corsham*, *Sonder*, *Utopia Project*, *Dream Well Writing*, *Corncrake Magazine* and Poetry Jukebox.

ANGELA GRAHAM is from Belfast and lives in Northern Ireland and Wales. *Sanctuary: There Must Be Somewhere* was published by Seren Books in 2022. Her short story collection, *A City*

*Burning,* came out in 2020 and was longlisted for the Edge Hill Short Story Prize. She is an award-winning tv and film producer.

MIM GREENE is a transpersonal therapist and poet from Drogheda. She is the daughter of the Patrick Kavanagh Award winner Angela Greene. She has contributed to Sublimer wishes on Lyric FM and was interviewed for American radio discussing the spiritual elements of her own poetry. She was included in *Washing Windows Too*. She happily resides in Portobello with her kitty muse Kismet!

ANITA GREG was born in London and came to Belfast to run a shop in the North Street Arcade selling pagan oddments and never looked back. She likes walking in bad weather, mythology, painting and bees. Published in the *Honest Ulsterman, Abridged, Forxfour* and the Waterways Festival booklet, she has also written a play about Emily Brontë, Emily Dickinson and a murder in a carriage which, strangely, has never been produced.

SINÉAD GRIFFIN has been published in *Poetry Ireland Review*, the *Honest Ulsterman, Skylight 47, Channel Literary Magazine*, the *Irish Times* New Irish Writing, the *Waxed Lemon*, the *Milk House*, the *Storms* journal and elsewhere. Winner of the Trócaire Poetry Ireland Competition 2021 (adult unpublished category), Pushcart nominated 2022, two chapbooks highly commended in the Fool for Poetry Prize 2022, shortlisted in the Fish Poetry Prize and South Dublin Libraries Poetry Prize, longlisted for Cúirt Poetry Prize and Bray Literary Festival Poetry Prize. Her poems have appeared in various anthologies.

SHARON GUARD completed an MA in Creative Writing at the University of Limerick. She writes mostly short stories and is working on a novel. She was the winner of the Molly Keane Creative Writing Award 2020 and has had stories and poetry listed in other competitions. Her short story 'Communion' was published in New Irish Writing in the *Irish Independent* in January 2023.

CHRISTINE HAMMOND began writing poetry whilst studying English at Queen's University Belfast. Her early poems were published in *The Gown* and *Women's News* where, as one of the original members, she also wrote arts reviews and was published in *Spare Rib*. Her poetry has been featured in anthologies including *The Poet's Place* and *Movement* (Community Arts Partnership), *The Female Line* (NI Women's Rights Movement), *The Sea* (Rebel Poetry Ireland), *Washing Windows, Too* and *III*, and *Her Other Language* (Arlen House). She is currently working on her first collection.

RACHEL HANDLEY is a poet, science fiction author and an academic philosopher based in Dublin. Their poetry has been published by *Poetry Ireland Review*, the *Liminal Review*, Arlen House, and *The Storms*, among others. She was nominated for the Pushcart Prize, longlisted for the BSFA Best Short Fiction Prize, and shortlisted for the South Dublin Libraries Poetry Competition. Their debut short story collection, *Possible Worlds and Other Stories*, was published by Ellipsis Imprints in 2022.

PHYL HERBERT was born in Dublin and worked for many years as an English and drama teacher in prison schools and in Liberties College. In 2008 she achieved an M.Phil in Creative Writing from TCD. It was only then that she started to write. She has since published a debut collection of short stories, *The Price of Desire* (Arlen House, 2016) and an essay in *Look! It's a Woman Writer!* (Arlen House, 2021). Her memoir, *The Price of Silence*, was published in 2023.

FLORENCE HEYHOE is a poet and textile artist living in County Down, by the shore of Carlingford Lough. She has been writing poetry for a decade but for the last four years the haibun form is her focus. Her work has been anthologised and published in journals in Ireland, the UK, India, America and Canada. With a keen eye for detail her inspiration comes from the landscape, family, friends and observing life. She is active on the blog Triveni Haiku India, where she has honed her skills under the guidance of the editorial team.

JENNIFER HORGAN is a poet living in Cork. Her work has been published in various online and print journals including *The*

*Honest Ulsterman, Ink Sweat and Tears* and *Howl: New Irish Writing*. Her debut poetry collection is due in 2025.

SACHA HUTCHINSON is a medical ophthalmologist who lives in Galway. Her poetry has appeared in poetry journals and anthologies including *ROPES, Skylight 47, The Storms, The Curlew, impspired, Lothlorien*. She was shortlisted for Over The Edge New Writer 2019. She won the Poems for Patience competition at Cuirt 2022.

JEAN JAMES was born in Northern Ireland, but lives in Swansea. She completed a Creative Writing MA at Swansea University with a focus on nature writing and poetry. Jean has published in *Abridged* and the *Welsh Arts Review*. She won The British Haiku Society haibun competition in 2013; came first and runner-up in the British Haiku Society tanka competition in 2015; and third in the Welsh Poetry Competition in 2018. A selection of her poems was published by Snapshot Press in 2019. In 2021 Hedgehog Press published *Bloom and Bones*, a collaboration with Welsh poet Rae Howells.

ROSEMARY JENKINSON is a playwright, poet and fiction writer from Belfast. In 2018 she received a Major Artist Award from ACNI. She was artist-in-residence at the Lyric Belfast 2017 and the Leuven Centre for Irish Studies 2019. Arlen House publish her plays *Billy Boy* and *Silent Trade*. Her short story collections are *Contemporary Problems Nos. 53 & 54*, *Aphrodite's Kiss*, *Catholic Boy* (shortlisted for the EU Prize for Literature), *Lifestyle Choice 10mgs* and *Marching Season*. Her latest collection *Love in the Time of Chaos* (Arlen House, 2023) was shortlisted for the Edge Hill Short Story Prize.

CATH-ANN KAVANAGH: I began writing poems and short stories in 2019. I am in the final stages of editing a novel. I reached second place in the Anthology Short Story Award 2021. In 2022, I joined a writer's workshop in Paris, followed by a writers' retreat facilitated by Claire Keegan in 2023.

HANNAH KIELY lives in Galway. Kiely has been published in Dedalus Press' *New Love Poems for Today*, *Vox Galvia: new Galway* writing, Galway Music Residency, RTÉ Sunday Miscellany, Pendemic.ie and Spilling Cocoa over Martin Amis, Waterford News & Star, Festive Star 2022 and Smashingtimes.ie. Kiely was a featured reader at Cúirt in 2016 in the Mná2016 Bardic Breakfast Series.

THERESE KIERAN lives in Belfast. Her work has appeared in many magazines and anthologies including the Honest Ulsterman, Apiary, FourXFour, Washing Windows, Coast to Coast to Coast, CAP, 26 Armistice 100 Days and Poetry Jukebox. She is a board member of Irish PEN and a professional member of the Irish Writers Centre and 26 Characters. In February 2023 her poems were published by Paekakariki Press in Dark Angels: Three Contemporary Poets Book One. In 2015 she was runner-up in the Poetry Ireland/Trocaire competition. She has received two ACNI SIAP awards.

BETHAN KILFOIL is originally from North Wales, and has lived in Newbridge, Co Kildare for many years. She works as a news journalist and writes in both Welsh and English.

SUSAN KNIGHT is author of six novels and three short story collections, including Out of Order (Arlen House, 2015). Recent books include her Mrs Hudson Investigates series of mysteries, involving Sherlock Holmes's landlady. Great fun to write. She lives in Dublin.

DONNA LEAMY is a scientist on a career break pursuing an MA in Creative Writing at UL. She previously won a placement on 'The Walls of Limerick' mentorship project, and is part of the UL Winter Writing School alumni. She is currently working on a memoir and accompanying poetry collection.

RÓISÍN LEGGETT BOHAN was chosen by Poetry Ireland for Introductions 2022. Her work appears in 'New Irish Writing', Southword, Poetry Ireland's ePub anthology among others. Her poems have been highly commended/shortlisted for the Allingham, Cúirt and Hammond House Award. In 2022 she was the Flash Fiction winner with Southword, the winner of CNF with Atlantic Currents II, and runner-up in the Martín Crawford Short Story Award and From the Well Short Story Award. The recipient of an Arts Council Agility Award, and Cork City Bursary, Róisín is also co-editor of *HOWL New Irish Writing*.

MARY LOCKHART: I'm a retired forensic investigator and daughter of farmer and shopkeeper/postmaster, where some of my characters come from. I write poetry, children's books, magic realism, short stories. I belong to the LexIcon creative writing group. The *Leitrim Guardian* published one of my short stories about village life as a child.

JACKIE LYNAM is from Dublin. Her poems have been published in *Washing Windows Too* and *III*, *The Covid Verses* (Paddler Press), the *Martello Journal*, the *Bangor Literary Journal*, *Honest Ulsterman* and *Boyne Berries*. She was shortlisted for the 2021 Anthony Cronin International Poetry Award, the 2018 Bangor Poetry Competition and Write by the Sea Competition. She has also written non-fiction pieces for the *Irish Independent* and RTÉ Radio One's Sunday Miscellany. *Traces*, a chapbook of her poetry and essays was published in 2023.

CARMEL LYNCH directed a Media Production course for the CDETB where she taught journalism and creative writing for many years. She also coordinated their extensive cultural programme which included, literary, Drama, photography, film and public speaking events. Her poetry was published in *Washing Windows Too*.

A native of Strokestown and living in Portumna, NOELLE LYNSKEY, poet and pharmacist, just completed her MA (Creative Writing) in UL. Selected as Strokestown's Poet in 2021 and working on her poetry collection, she also facilitates Portumna Pen Pushers and is artistic adviser to Shorelines Arts Festival. Readings include Cúirt, Clifden Arts Festival, RTÉ Sunday Miscellany, Dromineer Literary Festival, Lime Square Poets. Publications include *Staying Human*, the *Irish Times*, *Washing Windows Too*, *Local Wonders*, *Crannóg*, *Boyne Berries*, *Drawn to the Light*, *Romance Options* and *Skylight*.

SIOBHÁN MAC MAHON (MA Creative Writing, UCD) is a 'Word Witch' whose poetry speaks of the return of the Sacred Feminine and our deep connection to the earth. She's performed widely including the Southbank Centre, Stanza Poetry Festival, University of Vienna, Artemis International Festival – Spain, 100 Thousand Poets for Change, Italy and Festival Mná Summer 2023. A Hennessy winner, publications include *The Irish Times, Skylight 47, Hallelujah for 50 Foot Women* (Bloodaxe) and *Pride Poets*.

COLETTE MCANDREW: I was born in Oxfordshire and have lived in Antrim and Dublin. My interests are in the similarities and differences between places. My poems have been published in *Boyne Berries, A New Ulster* and by Arlen House. I have broadcast pieces for Lyric FM, included in their anthology *Ten Years of the Best of Irish Writing*.

CATHERINE MCCABE is supported by ACNI and The University of Atypical. Her work appears in *Her Other Language* (Arlen House, 2020) and *Washing Windows Too*. In 2022 she was shortlisted for Black Spring Press Group's Best of the Bottom Drawer Writing Prize for *Stiletto Heels & Moonshine*, her comic novel manuscript. She won Button Poetry's Short Form Poetry Contest in 2020 and was shortlisted for the Fly on the Wall Press Aryamati Poetry Prize 2020. In 2016, she co-authored a memoir for an ex-CIA informant, *The Black Market Concierge*.

MARY MCCARTHY holds an MA in Creative Writing from the University of Limerick where she graduated with First Class Honours. She was shortlisted for the Patrick Kavanagh Award in 2022. Her poetry has appeared in *Crossways Literary Magazine, Riverbed Review, Spirituality*, the *Southern Star*, the *Echo* and in the anthologies *Washing Windows Too, Chasing Shadows* and *A World Transformed*. She has completed two poetry collections and is working on her third.

HELEN MCCLEMENTS is a teacher, writer and blogger from Belfast. A regular at the Belfast storytelling event 'Tenx9', she appears frequently on their podcast, and several of her stories have been aired on BBC Radio Ulster's programme 'Tell Tales'. An excerpt from her upcoming memoir appeared in *Fortnight* in April 2022, and one of her poems featured in *Washing Windows Too*.

A first-generation Caribbean migrant, RAQUEL MCKEE applies a range of poetic styles to address personal and political issues to a number of audiences. She is a multi-disciplinary, multi-award-winning artist, who has poems published in collections in Ireland, the UK and in Jamaica, namely: *Four x Four Poetry Journal, The Corridor* xBorder edition; *Writing Home; Her Other Language; Fortnight; Lockdown Rhythms* & *JCDC* anthology 2022. She has performed at various festivals including the Cúirt International Festival of Literature. Raquel is a Poetry in Motion facilitator.

E.V. MCLOUGHLIN's writing has appeared in the *Blue Nib, Awkward Mermaid, Bangor Literary Journal, The Writer's Cafe, Rat's Ass Review, Honest Ulsterman, Wizards in Space* and several CAP anthologies. Her poems were longlisted for the Seamus Heaney Award for New Writing 2016 and shortlisted for the Fresher Writing Prize 2017. She loves walking by the sea, coffee, books, and city lights; and currently lives in County Antrim with her husband and son.

LIZ MCMANUS is a former TD and Government Minister of State. Winner of the Hennessy Short Story, Listowel and Irish PEN awards. Her novels include *Acts of Subversion* (Poolbeg), *A Shadow in the Yard* (Ward River) and, in 2023, her third novel, *When Things Come to Light,* was published by Arlen House.

I mBaile Átha Cliath a rugadh EILÍS NÍ ANLUAIN a bhfuil a saol fásta caite aici i mBré, Co. Chill Mhantain mar ar thóg sí clann. Colúnaí tráth leis an *Irish Times,* údar an úrscéil *Filleann Seoirse*, í ag obair faoi láthair mar aistritheoir sa Bhruiséil.

PATRICIA MAGUIRE: I am a Belfast girl. I have been writing poetry since I was 10. I love writing prose and poetry and oil painting, love language in all its myriad forms, love music and animals and being on my own. I lost Enda two years ago and miss her hugely. This poem is in honour of a friend who taught me on so many levels. When life knocks you or rocks you, you have to put pen to paper and when people make an imprint on your life you have a duty to set their essence in print if you can.

TRIONA MC MORROW lives in Dún Laoghaire. Shortlisted in the International Francis Ledwidge Poetry Competition 2009/2011/2013; the Galway University Hospital's Arts Trust poetry competition 2013 and the Rush poetry competition 2017. She has a poem published in *The Peoples' Acorn*, in the grounds of Áras an Uachtarain, commissioned by President Michael D. Higgins and Sabina Higgins in 2017. She has been published in *Cyphers, North West Words, Ibbetson Street* (Boston), *Bealtaine* and *Washing Windows Too*. Triona had a poem published in an exhibition curated by ArtnetDlr. She is a member of the Green Kites writing group.

MARI MAXWELL's work featured in *Washing Windows Too* and in the Poetry Jukebox STARS curation. She received a professional development award from the Arts Council and a Words Ireland/Mayo County Council mentorship. Her work has been shortlisted in: From The Well, Cork County Council, 2020/2017/2015; creativewritingink.co.uk 2019; Walking on Thin Ice: Writers Fighting Back Against Stigma and Institutional Power 2014. Third in the Cathal Buí Blacklion Poetry Competition 2019; Second place poetry Dromineer Literary Festival 2015, second place short story 2008. She was longlisted for the *RTÉ Guide* Penguin Short Story 2015 and Highly Commended in the Francis Ledwidge International Poetry Festival 2018/2014.

AMANDA MOLONEY is a writer from Limerick. A former bookshop manager and current student on the Creative Writing MA in UL. She has been published in the Women's Collective *Untold Stories* and *Astronomy Ireland* magazine.

SONYA MULLIGAN is a director, producer, poet, painter and crafter. She is the host of Pride Poets, a monthly poetry night. *Outitude: the Irish Lesbian Community* which she directed is her first feature documentary and won a number of audience awards and a Community Visibility Award.

MITZIE MURPHY has a BSc in Psychotherapy, Dip in Expressive Arts Therapy and an MA in Creative Writing. Her poetry has been published in *Washing Windows Too* and by Poetry Day

Ireland. One of her short stories was published in the *Irish Times*. Mitzie's poetry was shortlisted for Cracked Anvil and longlisted for Bridport.

ANNE MURRAY is a keen family historian and enjoys writing creative memoir. She is currently taking a class at QUB exploring the use of ekphrasis to write poetry and prose, particularly in response to art treasures housed in the Ulster Museum. Anne has been published in Women Aloud NI's book of short stories and poems, *North Star*.

BRÍD NÍ CHOMÁIN is a writer from Dublin. Her short story, 'Missing', was included in an anthology from Roddy Doyle's initiative, Fighting Words, also featuring in the *Irish Times* magazine. Her recent play, *Clearance* (co-written with Síofra O'Meara) received mentorship from Fishamble and saw her placed on the Fringe Lab 50 to Watch list.

CIARA NÍ É, bilingual poet, performer, playwright and screenwriter. The founder of REIC, a monthly multilingual spoken word event and co-founder of LGBTQ+ arts collective *AerachAiteachGaelach*. Chosen as one of the *Irish Examiner*'s '100 Women Changing Ireland in 2022' and an Irish Writers Centre ambassador. 2023 Artist in Residence with UCD Scoil ICSF, previously with the Dublin Fringe Festival and DCU. Has performed in New York, London, Brussels, Sweden and across Ireland. Published in anthologies *Bone and Marrow/Cnámh agus Smior*, *Queering the Green*, *Washing Windows Too* and *III*, *Aneas*, *Icarus* and *Comhar*. Her first collection is forthcoming.

HELENA NOLAN is a Patrick Kavanagh Award winner and was shortlisted for the Hennessy, Strokestown and Fish awards. She holds an MA in Creative Writing from UCD and is widely published in anthologies and journals, including in *Washing Windows Too* and *Poetry Ireland Review*. As Consul General of Ireland in New York, she has a focus on cultural diplomacy and loves to support Irish writers and artists, especially less-known voices. Helena is co-editor of *All Strangers Here* (Arlen House).

Originally from Donegal, Irish artist and poet MARIA NOONAN-MCDERMOTT now lives and works from her studio in Kinlough, County Leitrim. Heavily influenced by the impressionist movement, her work focuses on the study of light and form in Irish landscapes. She qualified and worked in the fashion industry before returning to study Fine Art at the University of Ulster. To date, she has participated in 24 solo exhibitions and numerous group exhibitions, both nationally and internationally.

GRACE O'DOHERTY is from Wicklow and is currently based in Berlin. Her poetry has been published in *Washing Windows Too: Irish Women Write Poetry*, *Poetry Bus*, *Poetry Ireland Review*, *Banshee*, *Honest Ulsterman*, *Stony Thursday Book* and *My Kinsale: An Anthology*. In 2022 she attended the Poetry Summer School at the Seamus Heaney Centre and participated in the Gallery autumn workshop series. She was one of ten poets selected for a masterclass and reading with Paul Muldoon at Kinsale Arts Weekend 2022.

LAUREN O'DONOVAN is from Cork. In 2023 she won the Patrick Kavanagh Award and the Cúirt New Writing Prize, and was shortlisted/runner-up for Listowel Writers' Week Collection Award, Poetry Business Book & Pamphlet Competition, Fool For Poetry Chapbook Competition and the Fish Poetry Prize. Lauren is co-founder of Lime Square Poets, an editor at *HOWL New Irish Writing* and is currently working on her debut collection.

BLAITHIN O'REILLY MURPHY is author of the following published works: *Distinctive Weddings, Tying the Knot without the Rope Burns*, *Sealed with a Christmas Kiss* [More than Mistletoe], *Sausage Rolls for Everyone* [The Mistletoe Mixtape]. She has previously been shortlisted for the Penguin Christmas Love Story Competition. She resides in Lusk.

SARAH PADDEN is an Irish-descent Yorkshire lass who lives in Galway. Her poetry reflects on the migrant experience, landscapes and being at home or being Other, in different cultures and countries. Sarah's poetry has previously been published in the *Washing Windows* anthologies, *Skylight 47*, *ROPES*, *A New Ulster*, *Freehand*. She was selected as a featured reader at Over the Edge 2019 and the 2020 Cuirt Literary Festival New Writers showcase. Sarah was a former winner of the Galway Poetry slam and was shortlisted for the 2023 Saolta Arts Poems for Patience competition.

CELINA PAPENDORF is pursuing an MA in Creative Writing at the University of Limerick, where she is currently working on her debut novel. She moved to Ireland from Germany, where she completed a BA in Art History, and worked for an online newspaper and published her poetry.

SAAKSHI PATEL earned an MA in Poetry with distinction from QUB. She was awarded the Seamus Heaney Centre International Scholarship, the 2021 Ireland Chair of Poetry Student Award and the John Hewitt International Summer School Bursary. Her poems have been published in *The Best Asian Poetry 2021* by Kitaab, *Local Wonders* (Dedalus), *Washing Windows Too* and *III*, *AHVAAZ* by the League of Canadian Poets, *Catatonic Daughters*, the *Honest Ulsterman* and *yolk* literary journal. She was featured in Breaking Ground Ireland 2022, a Cúirt International Festival of Literature project.

RUTH QUINLAN is originally from Kerry but now lives in Galway. She has been selected for a Heinrich Böll Cottage Writer Residency, the Cork Poetry Festival Introductions, and the Poetry Ireland Introductions series. She has won awards for both poetry and fiction and is co-editor of *Skylight 47*.

MARY RINGLAND lives in County Down and works as a teacher. She has been longlisted and shortlisted for the Annual Bangor Poetry Competition 2020. Her work has appeared in three *Washing Windows* anthologies and *Her Other Language* (Arlen House, 2022); the *Bangor Literary Journal*, CAP anthologies and *Romance Options* (Dedalus, 2022).

REBECCA RUANE is an artist from Galway. Her work has been published in *Skylight47*, *Stony Thursday*, *WordCityLit*, used as an audio piece (Quare festival) and she has given readings at Over The Edge and The Hall of The Red Earl. She has received mentorships from Keith Payne, Mary Madec and Kevin Higgins.

D'OR SEIFER lives in Limerick. Her work has appeared in *Shearsman, The Banyan Review, Abridged, Ink Sweat & Tears, Skylight 47*, Dedalus Press's *Romance Options* anthology and more. D'or co-runs the online series Lime Square Poets and Limerick's in-person First Wednesday Series. She recently joined Skylight 47's editing team.

MARY SHANNON is from Belfast; her poetry has appeared in various anthologies. 'Nesting for Nainsí' was featured on the Poetry Jukebox 2023. Her monologue 'A Partridge in a Pear Tree' was screened online by the Waterside Theatre, 2020 and her poem Burning the Kelp won the Heather Newcombe Award 2019.

KATIE SHEEHAN lives in County Clare and works as a social researcher. Her work has appeared in magazines such as *Poetry Ireland Review* and *Southword*, and was recognised in Poetry Ireland's Introductions Series. Her first collection, *Poplar*, is forthcoming with Salmon Poetry.

CASSIE SMITH-CHRISTMAS lives in Galway. Her novel, *The Absence of Light,* was a winner in the Irish Writers Centre Novel Fair 2023. Her creative writing has appeared in journals such as *Southword; Aimsir; Crannóg; Causeway/ Cabhsair; The New Word Order; The Milk House; The Wild Word; Gutter; Poets' Republic* and *Earthlines*.

AMY SMYTH is from Dundalk. The signing of the Good Friday Agreement when she was 8 had a profound effect on how she viewed peace and the power of forgiveness. Amy is a diplomat who lives in Belfast with her finance Kevin and dog Friday – named after the Good Friday Agreement. Amy is also dyslexic and is a passionate advocate for people with disabilities and the LGBTQ community in her free time.

EILIS STANLEY lives in Ashford, County Wicklow. She has won a number of poetry awards including Bridport, Listowel First Prize Single Poem, Listowel International Poetry Collection Prize, and has been shortlisted for the Fish, Strokestown and Hennessy awards. Her poems have been published in anthologies and magazines including Bridport, Listowel, *Poetry Ireland Review* and *Washing Window Too*. She has recently completed her first poetry collection.

SARAH STRONG is a visual artist and poet, born in 1949 in Dublin to an Irish Catholic mother and English Protestant father. Her poems appear in *Southword, London Grip, Silver Stream, Washing Windows, Washing Windows Too, Washing Windows III, Prodding the Pelt, South Bank Poetry*. She was shortlisted for Fire River poetry competition (2016). She has read at City Lit. Talks Back, Camden Poets. Her exhibition *Washing Soot off Stained Glass: Poetry and Art with Eithne Strong and Sarah Strong* was held in autumn 2023 at Maynooth University in tandem with MoLI.

LILA STUART lives in Belfast. Her poems have been published in *Washing Windows, Burren Insight, CAP anthologies, Her Other Language, Corncrake*.

CSILLA TOLDY is a writer and translator from Hungary. Her writing appears in magazines and anthologies and in three poetry pamphlets: *Red Roots – Orange Sky* (2013), *The Emigrant Woman's Tale* (2015) and *Vertical Montage* (2018), as short fiction in *Angel Fur and Other Stories* (2019) and as a novel, *Bed Table Door* (2023). Csilla creates film poems as a visual artist. Her award-winning work has been screened at international festivals. Her first full collection of poetry is forthcoming.

ENYA TROFIMOFF is a Mexican author, currently living in Limerick, specialising in fantasy stories centered on key themes such as friendship, love, good turned evil, and loss of innocence. She has been writing poems since the summer of 2020 and is a novice sonneteer.

CARMEL UÍ CHEALLAIGH has had nine children's books published, including picture books *as Gaeilge* and Irish centenary history titles for ages 8+. She retired recently from her post as Senior Executive Librarian in the LexIcon Library, having spent forty years working in the Dún Laoghaire Rathdown Library Service.

EMI UYEMATSU has been writing professionally since the age of nineteen and is an author of fiction and poetry. An American currently living and studying in Ireland, this is Emi's first contribution to a poetry collection and first time appearing in print.

MORGAN L. VENTURA is a writer and curator based in Belfast whose poetry appears in *Banshee*, *Romance Options* (Dedalus), the *Honest Ulsterman* and *Shoreline of Infinity*, whilst prose appears in *Best Canadian Essays 2021*, *The Magazine of Fantasy and Science Fiction* and *Lackington's*. Morgan holds a PhD in Anthropology from the University of Chicago and a MA in Poetry from the Seamus Heaney Centre.

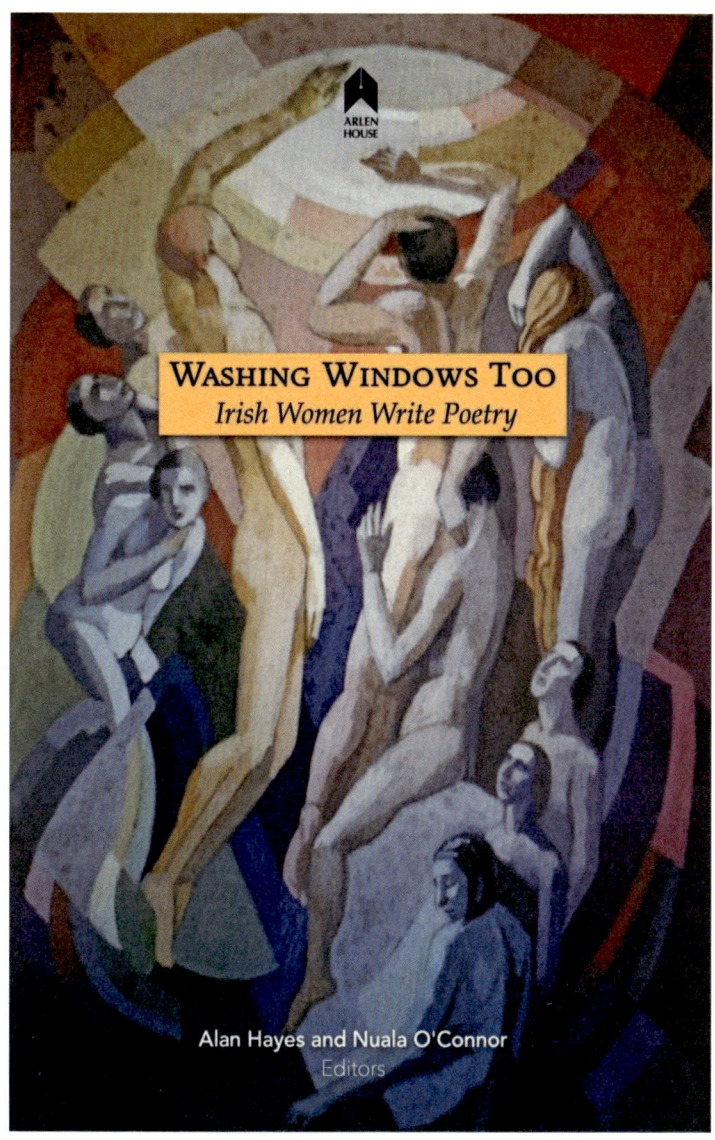

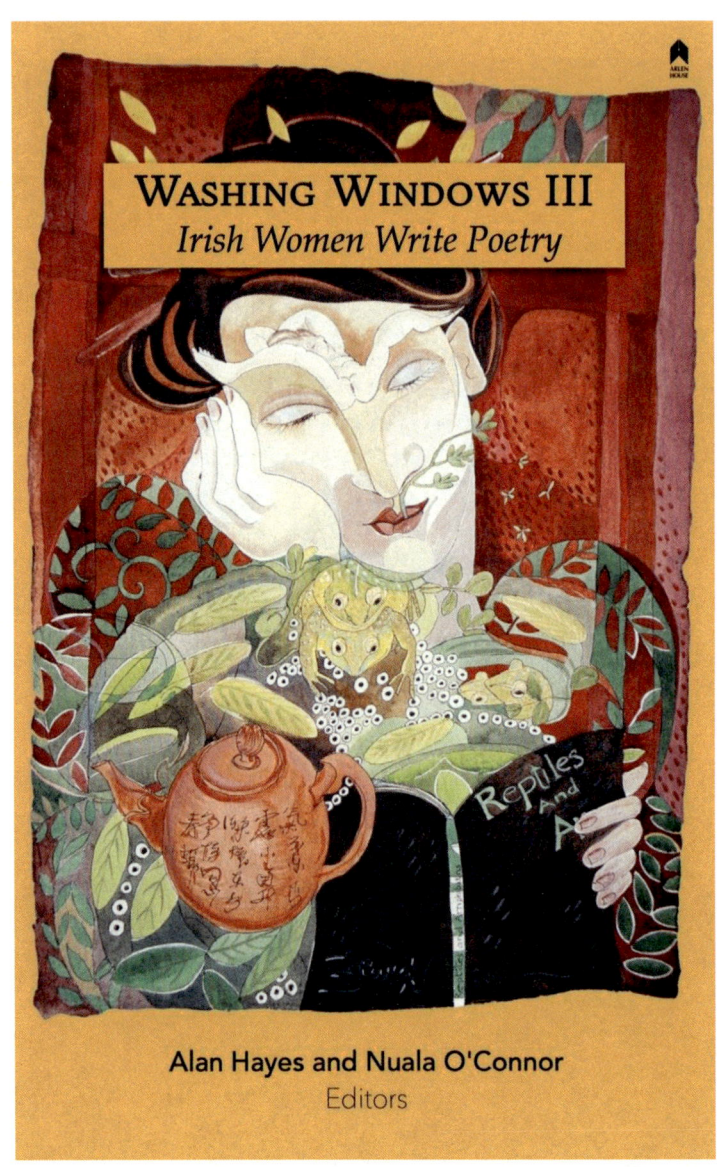